P9-CBK-460

CONFRONTING GLOBAL WARMING

The Role of the Individual

Confronting Global Warming

The Role of the Individual

Rebecca Ferguson

Michael E. Mann
Consulting Editor

GREENHAVEN PRESS
A part of Gale, Cengage Learning

GALE
CENGAGE Learning

Detroit • New York • San Francisco • New Haven, Conn • Waterville, Maine • London

GALE
CENGAGE Learning™

Christine Nasso, *Publisher*
Elizabeth Des Chenes, *Managing Editor*

© 2011 Greenhaven Press, a part of Gale, Cengage Learning

For more information, contact:

Greenhaven Press
27500 Drake Rd.
Farmington Hills, MI 48331-3535
Or you can visit our Internet site at
gale.cengage.com.

For product information and technology assistance, contact us at
Gale Customer Support, 1-800-877-4253.
For permission to use material from this text or product, submit all requests online at
www.cengage.com/permissions.
Further permissions questions can be e-mailed to
permissionrequest@cengage.com

Every effort is made to ensure that Greenhaven Press accurately reflects the original intent of the authors. Every effort has been made to trace the owners of copyrighted material.

Cover Image copyright JinYoung Lee, 2010. Used under license from Shutterstock.com and Dmitry Shironosov/Shutterstock.com; Leaf icon © iStockPhoto.com/domin_domin.

**LIBRARY OF CONGRESS
CATALOGING-IN-PUBLICATION DATA**
Ferguson, Rebecca.
 The role of the individual / Rebecca Ferguson.
  p. cm. -- (Confronting global warming)
 Includes bibliographical references and index.
 ISBN 978-0-7377-4853-6 (hardcover)
 1. Environmentalism. 2. Sustainable living. 3. Global warming--Prevention. I. Title.
  GE195.F47 2011
  333.72--dc22
                                    2010030743

Printed in the United States of America
1 2 3 4 5 6 7 15 14 13 12 11

Contents

Preface

> *"The warnings about global warming*
> *have been extremely clear for a long*
> *time. We are facing a global climate*
> *crisis. It is deepening. We are entering*
> *a period of consequences."*
> *Al Gore*

Still hotly debated by some, human-induced global warming is now accepted in the scientific community. Earth's average yearly temperature is getting steadily warmer; sea levels are rising due to melting ice caps; and the resulting impact on ocean life, wildlife, and human life is already evident. The human-induced buildup of greenhouse gases in the atmosphere poses serious and diverse threats to life on earth. As scientists work to develop accurate models to predict the future impact of global warming, researchers, policy makers, and industry leaders are coming to terms with what can be done today to halt and reverse the human contributions to global climate change.

Each volume in the Confronting Global Warming series examines the current and impending challenges the planet faces because of global warming. Several titles focus on a particular aspect of life—such as weather, farming, health, or nature and wildlife—that has been altered by climate change. Consulting the works of leading experts in the field, Confronting Global Warming authors present the current status of those aspects as they have been affected by global warming, highlight key future challenges, examine potential solutions for dealing with the results of climate change, and address the pros and cons of imminent changes and challenges. Other volumes in the series—such as those dedicated to the role of government, the role of industry, and the role of the individual—address the impact various facets of society can have on climate change. The result is a series that provides students and general-interest readers with a solid understanding of the worldwide ramifications of climate change and what can be done to help humanity adapt to changing conditions and mitigate damage.

Each volume includes:

- A descriptive **table of contents** listing subtopics, charts, graphs, maps, and sidebars included in each chapter
- Full-color **charts, graphs, and maps** to illustrate key points, concepts, and theories
- Full-color **photos** that enhance textual material
- **Sidebars** that provide explanations of technical concepts or statistical information, present case studies to illustrate the international impact of global warming, or offer excerpts from primary and secondary documents
- **Pulled quotes** containing key points and statistical figures
- A **glossary** providing users with definitions of important terms
- An annotated **bibliography** of additional books, periodicals, and Web sites for further research
- A detailed **subject index** to allow users to quickly find the information they need

The Confronting Global Warming series provides students and general-interest readers with the information they need to understand the complex issue of climate change. Titles in the series offer users a well-rounded view of global warming, presented in an engaging format. Confronting Global Warming not only provides context for how society has dealt with climate change thus far but also encapsulates debates about how it will confront issues related to climate in the future.

Foreword

Earth's climate is a complex system of interacting natural components. These components include the atmosphere, the ocean, and the continental ice sheets. Living things on earth—or, the biosphere—also constitute an important component of the climate system.

Natural Factors Cause Some of Earth's Warming and Cooling

Numerous factors influence Earth's climate system, some of them natural. For example, the slow drift of continents that takes place over millions of years, a process known as plate tectonics, influences the composition of the atmosphere through its impact on volcanic activity and surface erosion. Another significant factor involves naturally occurring gases in the atmosphere, known as greenhouse gases, which have a warming influence on Earth's surface. Scientists have known about this warming effect for nearly two centuries: These gases absorb outgoing heat energy and direct it back toward the surface. In the absence of this natural greenhouse effect, Earth would be a frozen, and most likely lifeless, planet.

Another natural factor affecting Earth's climate—this one measured on timescales of several millennia—involves cyclical variations in the geometry of Earth's orbit around the sun. These variations alter the distribution of solar radiation over the surface of Earth and are responsible for the coming and going of the ice ages every one hundred thousand years or so. In addition, small variations in the brightness of the sun drive minor changes in Earth's surface temperature over decades and centuries. Explosive volcanic activity, such as the Mount Pinatubo eruption in the Philippines in 1991, also affects Earth's climate. These eruptions inject highly reflective particles called aerosol into the upper part of the atmosphere, known as the stratosphere, where they can reside for a year or longer. These particles reflect some of the incoming sunlight back into space and cool Earth's surface for years at a time.

Human Progress Puts Pressure on Natural Climate Patterns

Since the dawn of the industrial revolution some two centuries ago, however, humans have become the principal drivers of climate change. The burning of fossil fuels—such as oil, coal, and natural gas—has led to an increase in atmospheric levels of carbon dioxide, a powerful greenhouse gas. And farming practices have led to increased atmospheric levels of methane, another potent greenhouse gas. If humanity continues such activities at the current rate through the end of this century, the concentrations of greenhouse gases in the atmosphere will be higher than they have been for tens of millions of years. It is the unprecedented rate at which we are amplifying the greenhouse effect, warming Earth's surface, and modifying our climate that causes scientists so much concern.

The Role of Scientists in Climate Observation and Projection

Scientists study Earth's climate not just from observation but also from a theoretical perspective. Modern-day climate models successfully reproduce the key features of Earth's climate, including the variations in wind patterns around the globe, the major ocean current systems such as the Gulf Stream, and the seasonal changes in temperature and rainfall associated with Earth's annual revolution around the sun. The models also reproduce some of the more complex natural oscillations of the climate system. Just as the atmosphere displays random day-to-day variability that we term "weather," the climate system produces its own random variations, on timescales of years. One important example is the phenomenon called El Niño, a periodic warming of the eastern tropical Pacific Ocean surface that influences seasonal patterns of temperature and rainfall around the globe. The ability to use models to reproduce the climate's complicated natural oscillatory behavior gives scientists increased confidence that these models are up to the task of mimicking the climate system's response to human impacts.

To that end, scientists have subjected climate models to a number of rigorous tests of their reliability. James Hansen of the NASA Goddard Institute for Space Studies performed a famous experiment back in 1988, when he subjected a climate model (one relatively primitive by modern standards) to possible future fossil fuel emissions scenarios. For the scenario that most closely matches actual emissions since then, the model's predicted course of global temperature increase shows an uncanny correspondence to the actual increase in temperature over the intervening two decades. When Mount Pinatubo erupted in the Philippines in 1991, Hansen performed another famous experiment. Before the volcanic aerosol had an opportunity to influence the climate (it takes several months to spread globally throughout the atmosphere), he took the same climate model and subjected it to the estimated atmospheric aerosol distribution. Over the next two years, actual global average surface temperatures proceeded to cool a little less than 1°C (1.8°F), just as Hansen's model predicted they would.

Given that there is good reason to trust the models, scientists can use them to answer important questions about climate change. One such question weighs the human factors against the natural factors to determine responsibility for the dramatic changes currently taking place in our climate. When driven by natural factors alone, climate models do not reproduce the observed warming of the past century. Only when these models are also driven by human factors—primarily, the increase in greenhouse gas concentrations—do they reproduce the observed warming. Of course, the models are not used just to look at the past. To make projections of future climate change, climate scientists consider various possible scenarios or pathways of future human activity.

The earth has warmed roughly 1°C since preindustrial times. In the "business as usual" scenario, where we continue the current course of burning fossil fuel through the twenty-first century, models predict an additional warming anywhere from roughly 2°C to 5°C (3.6°F to 9°F). The models also show that even if we were to stop fossil fuel burning today, we are probably committed to as much as 0.6°C additional warming because of the inertia of the climate system. This inertia ensures warming for a century to come, simply due to our greenhouse gas emissions thus far. This committed warming introduces a profound procrastination penalty for not taking immediate action. If we are to avert an additional warming of 1°C, which would bring the net warming to 2°C—often considered an appropriate threshold for defining dangerous human impact on our climate—we have to act almost immediately.

Long-Term Warming May Bring About Extreme Changes Worldwide

In the "business as usual" emissions scenario, climate change will have an array of substantial impacts on our society and the environment by the end of this century. Patterns of rainfall and drought are projected to shift in such a way that some regions currently stressed for water resources, such as the desert southwest of the United States and the Middle East, are likely to become drier. More intense rainfall events in other regions, such as Europe and the midwestern United States, could lead to increased flooding. Heat waves like the one in Europe in summer 2003, which killed more than thirty thousand people, are projected to become far more common. Atlantic hurricanes are likely to reach greater intensities, potentially doing far more damage to coastal infrastructure.

Furthermore, regions such as the Arctic are expected to warm faster than the rest of the globe. Disappearing Arctic sea ice already threatens wildlife, including polar bears and walruses. Given another 2°C warming (3.6°F), a substantial portion of the

Greenland ice sheet is likely to melt. This event, combined with other factors, could lead to more than 1 meter (about 3 feet) of sea-level rise by the end of the century. Such a rise in sea level would threaten many American East Coast and Gulf Coast cities, as well as low-lying coastal regions and islands around the world. Food production in tropical regions, already insufficient to meet the needs of some populations, will probably decrease with future warming. The incidence of infectious disease is expected to increase in higher elevations and in latitudes with warming temperatures. In short, the impacts of future climate change are likely to have a devastating impact on society and our environment in the absence of intervention.

Strategies for Confronting Climate Change

Options for dealing with the threats of climate change include both adaptation to inevitable changes and mitigation, or lessening, of those changes that we can still affect. One possible adaptation would be to adjust our agricultural practices to the changing regional patterns of temperature and rainfall. Another would be to build coastal defenses against the inundation from sea-level rise. Only mitigation, however, can prevent the most threatening changes. One means of mitigation that has been given much recent attention is geoengineering. This method involves perturbing the climate system in such a way as to partly or fully offset the warming impact of rising greenhouse gas concentrations. One geoengineering approach involves periodically shooting aerosol particles, similar to ones produced by volcanic eruptions, into the stratosphere—essentially emulating the cooling impact of a major volcanic eruption on an ongoing basis. As with nearly all geoengineering proposals, there are potential perils with this scheme, including an increased tendency for continental drought and the acceleration of stratospheric ozone depletion.

The only foolproof strategy for climate change mitigation is the decrease of greenhouse gas emissions. If we are to avert a dangerous 2°C increase relative to preindustrial times, we will probably need to bring greenhouse gas emissions to a peak within the coming years and reduce them well below current levels within the coming decades. Any strategy for such a reduction of emissions must be international and multipronged, involving greater conservation of energy resources; a shift toward alternative, carbon-free sources of energy; and a coordinated set of governmental policies that encourage responsible corporate and individual practices. Some contrarian voices argue that we cannot afford to take such steps. Actually, given the procrastination penalty of not acting on the climate change problem, what we truly cannot afford is to delay action.

Evidently, the problem of climate change crosses multiple disciplinary boundaries and involves the physical, biological, and social sciences. As an issue facing all of civilization, climate change demands political, economic, and ethical considerations. With the Confronting Global Warming series, Greenhaven Press addresses all of these considerations in an accessible format. In ten thorough volumes, the series covers the full range of climate change impacts (water and ice; extreme weather; population, resources, and conflict; nature and wildlife; farming and food supply; health and disease) and the various essential components of any solution to the climate change problem (energy production and alternative energy; the role of government; the role of industry; and the role of the individual). It is my hope and expectation that this series will become a useful resource for anyone who is curious about not only the nature of the problem but also about what we can do to solve it.

Michael E. Mann

Michael E. Mann is a professor in the Department of Meteorology at Penn State University and director of the Penn State Earth System

Science Center. In 2002 he was selected as one of the fifty lead-ing visionaries in science and technology by Scientific American. *He was a lead author for the "Observed Climate Variability and Change" chapter of the Intergovernmental Panel on Climate Change (IPCC) Third Scientific Assessment Report, and in 2007 he shared the Nobel Peace Prize with other IPCC authors. He is the author of more than 120 peer-reviewed publications, and he recently coauthored the book* Dire Predictions: Understanding Global Warming *with colleague Lee Kump. Mann is also a co-founder and avid contributor to the award-winning science Web site RealClimate.org.*

CHAPTER 1

Carbon Footprints and Why They Matter

There is a lot of talk today about carbon footprints. Although the term refers to the amount of carbon dioxide (CO_2) that a human activity releases into Earth's atmosphere, it has become shorthand for discussing the negative environmental impact of an individual, household, or business. Several organizations offer calculators on their Web sites for determining carbon footprint, or the carbon dioxide emissions produced by an individual or household based on input the user provides. While this is a useful calculation, it is equally important to understand why it matters. It is also important to understand the other kinds of human-made emissions that contribute to global warming; carbon dioxide is just one of several greenhouse gases, gases that are accumulating in Earth's atmosphere and, according to climate experts, contributing to rising global temperatures.

The Case for Global Warming

In March 2007, the United Nations' Intergovernmental Panel on Climate Change (IPCC), led by U.S. government scientist Susan Solomon, concluded in a report that "warming of the climate system is unequivocal."[1] The IPCC report summarized the conclu-

---

Following page: Cars in Linfen, China, and throughout the world contribute to greenhouse gas emissions. Combustion of fossil fuels such as oil is the largest source of human-made carbon dioxide emissions, according to the U.S. Environmental Protection Agency. Qilai Shen/ Bloomberg via Getty Images.

sions reached during an international meeting of climate experts in Paris, France. The group of scientists who met at the IPCC conference expressed 90 percent certainty that global warming is caused by the buildup of greenhouse gases in the earth's atmosphere. In short, human activities were linked to global warming, making headlines around the world. The IPCC summary report further stated that warming is "now evident from observations of increases in global average air and ocean temperatures, widespread melting of snow and ice, and rising global average sea level."[2]

Consensus around these conclusions—that the earth is warming and that humans are responsible for it—steadily mounted, bolstered by former U.S. vice president Al Gore's bestselling book and acclaimed documentary, *An Inconvenient Truth* (2006). In October 2007, the IPCC and Gore were named as the recipients of the Nobel Peace Prize, "for their efforts to build up and disseminate greater knowledge about manmade climate change, and to lay the foundations for the measures that are needed to counteract such change."[3] Still, some scientists disputed the conclusions reached by the IPCC and Gore, claiming that the data lacked integrity or that natural processes were causing global warming.

While denialists argue that consensus does not equal science, many measurements indicate that the earth is warming— that the data are, in fact, solid. According to NASA's Goddard Institute of Space Studies, the ten warmest years on earth all occurred within the twelve-year period from 1997 through 2008. During the twentieth century, average global temperatures rose by 1.3°F (0.74°C)—and while that may seem like an insignificant increase, climatologists and environmentalists point to it as a contributing factor in extreme weather conditions such as hurricanes and drought, the loss of habitats and consequent extinction of species, and the rising acidity of oceans and consequent bleaching of coral reefs. Furthermore, that 1.3°F increase is only the *average* rise in global temperatures; temperatures are rising more dramatically in certain regions. According to the nonprofit

Natural Resources Defense Council, average temperatures in the Arctic are rising twice as fast as they are elsewhere in the world.[4] Because of rising temperatures, Arctic ice is getting thinner, breaking apart, and melting. NASA's satellite images of the North Pole confirm that the ice cap there is shrinking, at a rate of about 9 percent each decade.

The Antarctic ice sheet is similarly threatened by melting. In August 2009 a group of British scientists announced study results indicating that the Pine Island Glacier, one of the largest in the West Antarctic ice sheet (WAIS), is thinning four times faster than it was ten years ago. One of the study's authors, Andrew Shepherd of Leeds University (United Kingdom), remarked on the findings, saying "Nothing in the natural world is lost at an accelerating exponential rate like this glacier."[5] American physicist and climate expert Joseph Romm explains rapid melt this way:

> The warmer it gets, the more unstable WAIS outlet glaciers will become. Since so much of the ice sheet is grounded underwater, rising sea levels may have the effect of lifting the sheets, allowing more—and increasingly warmer—water underneath it, leading to further bottom melting, more ice shelf disintegration, accelerated glacial flow, and further sea level rise.[6]

Furthermore, in 2009 in the journal *Nature*, researchers published the results of a study that looked at Antarctic dirt cores—the first results of a $30 million multinational Antarctic drilling program, largely funded by the U.S. National Science Foundation. Scientists said the core samples they studied show that the massive West Antarctic ice sheet regularly melted about every forty thousand years during a period when the climate was about 5°F (3 to 4.5°C) warmer than now and carbon dioxide levels were slightly higher than now. But these past melts coincided with regular changes in the Earth's tilt—changes that are not taking place today.

A March 2009 meeting of the International Scientific Congress on Climate Change in Copenhagen, Denmark, furthered the case for global warming, concluding that sea levels are rising even faster than the IPCC had predicted two years earlier. "The sea-level rise may well exceed one meter by 2100 if we continue on our path of increasing emissions,"[7] said Stefan Rahmstorf, professor at the Potsdam Institute for Climate Impact Research (Germany). The IPCC's earlier prediction had been that sea levels would rise between 18 and 59 centimeters (7 and 23 inches) this century. Other scientists echoed Rahmstorf's comment, warning that something must be done to curb emissions, or the Earth and its inhabitants will suffer the consequences.

Questions Raised by Global Warming Skeptics

One change in Antarctica would seem to support the denialists' argument against global warming: During the past twenty years, southern sea ice has increased overall. But in 2005, a NASA-funded study concluded that global warming may be producing a "counterintuitive phenomenon"[8] at the South Pole through snow-to-ice conversion. Using satellite observations, researchers were able to assess snow depth on sea ice and incorporate that data into precipitation models. Their conclusion, published in the June 2005 issue of the *Journal of Geophysical Research*, was that increased precipitation rates in the Antarctic have led to deeper snow, which becomes so heavy that it pushes ice below sea level, where snow cover refreezes as more ice.

Some skeptics of human-caused global warming wonder why temperatures are not rising steadily. Scientists point to natural variations to explain this phenomenon: Weather systems, such as El Niño (a periodic warming of surface waters in the eastern and central Pacific Ocean that causes unusual global weather patterns) and La Niña (a periodic cooling of the same Pacific waters, again resulting in unusual weather patterns), also influence temperatures.

Unusual cold fronts, such as the one that blanketed much of the southern United States in early 2010, routinely raise questions about the validity of global warming. But, as Gerald Meehl, a scientist at the National Center for Atmospheric Research remarked, unseasonably cold weather is "part of a natural variability. We'll still have record cold temperatures. We'll just have fewer of them."[9]

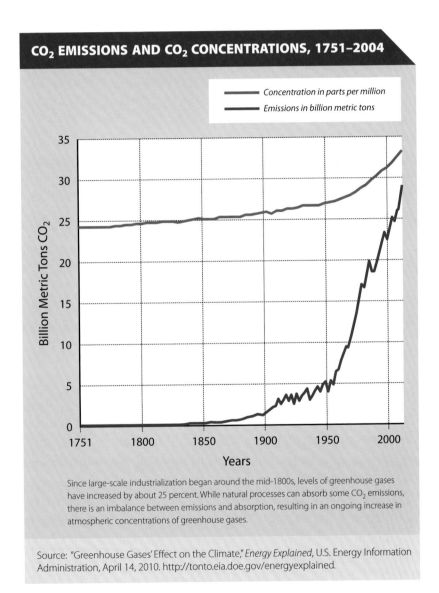

CO$_2$ EMISSIONS AND CO$_2$ CONCENTRATIONS, 1751–2004

Concentration in parts per million
Emissions in billion metric tons

Billion Metric Tons CO$_2$

Years

Since large-scale industrialization began around the mid-1800s, levels of greenhouse gases have increased by about 25 percent. While natural processes can absorb some CO$_2$ emissions, there is an imbalance between emissions and absorption, resulting in an ongoing increase in atmospheric concentrations of greenhouse gases.

Source: "Greenhouse Gases' Effect on the Climate," *Energy Explained*, U.S. Energy Information Administration, April 14, 2010. http://tonto.eia.doe.gov/energyexplained.

The Carbon Cycle

Some scientists argue that the carbon cycle—the movement of carbon between the atmosphere, land, and the ocean through natural processes such as photosynthesis—can absorb increased human-made carbon dioxide emissions. Others, however, note that not only have emissions increased, but the concentration of CO_2 in Earth's atmosphere has also increased since industrialization, from about 275 parts per million in the early eighteenth century to about 375 parts per million.[10] Humans have burned so much fuel that there is about 30 percent more carbon dioxide in the air today than there was about 150 years ago. According to the University Corporation for Atmospheric Research, a hub for research, education, and public outreach for the atmospheric and earth-system science community, ice cores reveal that the atmosphere has not held this much carbon for at least 420,000 years. According to this data, the carbon cycle is unable to absorb increased human-caused emissions.

Levels of several important greenhouse gases have increased by about 25 percent since large-scale industrialization began around 150 years ago.

The Greenhouse Effect

To understand the link between human activities and climate change, it is imperative to understand a group of chemical compounds climate experts call greenhouse gases. These gases absorb sunlight (infrared radiation) and trap the sun's heat in Earth's atmosphere. Greenhouse gases can occur naturally or they can be anthropogenic, made by humans. Since industrialization began in the mid-1700s, there has been a sharp increase in human-made greenhouse gases: carbon dioxide (CO_2), nitrogen oxide (NO_x), methane (CH_4), hydrofluorocarbons (HFCs), perfluorocarbons (PFCs), and sulfur hexafluoride

(SF$_6$). According to the measurements and analysis of the Oak Ridge National Laboratory and the U.S. Energy Information Administration (EIA), "Levels of several important greenhouse gases have increased by about 25 percent since large-scale industrialization began around 150 years ago."[11] Because these compounds are chiefly produced by humans through industrial processes, they are also called industrial gases. In the media they are often simply called emissions.

Where do these human-made greenhouse gases come from? According to the U.S. Environmental Protection Agency (EPA), the largest source of human-made carbon dioxide emissions globally is the combustion of fossil fuels such as coal, oil, and gas used in power plants, automobiles, trucks, jet engines, and industrial facilities. Carbon dioxide is also emitted by specialized production processes used in the mineral, metal, and petroleum industries. Deforestation is another contributor to carbon dioxide emissions: As trees and plants grow, they actually remove CO_2 from the atmosphere; as they are cut down, CO_2 emissions rise.

Nitrogen oxide is produced by humans through agricultural soil and manure management, sewage treatment, combustion of fossil fuel, and the production of certain acids. According to the EPA, the sources of human-made or human-influenced methane are landfills, natural gas systems, livestock digestive gases (through a process called enteric fermentation), manure management, wastewater treatment, petroleum systems, rice cultivation, abandoned coal mines, petrochemical production, iron and steel production, and the burning of agricultural residue (also called biomass).

Hydrofluorocarbons are human-made chemicals, many of which were developed as alternatives to ozone-depleting substances for industrial, commercial, and consumer products. Their main sources are air conditioning and refrigeration units.

Perfluorocarbons are produced by aluminum production and semiconductor manufacturing. The EPA explains that PFCs are particularly problematic as they are molecularly stable—"largely immune to the chemical processes in the lower atmosphere that break down most atmospheric pollutants. Not until the PFCs reach the mesosphere, about 60 kilometers above Earth, do very high-energy ultraviolet rays from the sun destroy them."[12]

Sulfur hexafluoride is a colorless, odorless, nontoxic, and nonflammable gas that is used for insulation and current interruption in electric power equipment, as well as in the magnesium industry, in semiconductor manufacturing, and as a tracer gas to detect leaks.

The GWP Factor

Although human emissions of hydrofluorocarbons, perfluorocarbons, and sulfur hexafluoride are relatively low when compared with carbon dioxide, nitrogen oxide, and methane emissions, they nevertheless play a critical role in contributing to the greenhouse effect. All three categories of these human-made compounds have been labeled high GWP gases—gases with the greatest global warming potential. Scientists developed the GWP concept so they can compare the ability of each greenhouse gas to trap heat in the atmosphere relative to another gas. The GWP for a particular greenhouse gas is the ratio of heat trapped by one unit mass of the greenhouse gas to that of one unit mass of CO_2 over a specified time period (often one hundred years). Using this international standard, in which carbon is the yardstick for measuring the warming potential of another substance, CO_2 is assigned a value of 1, and the warming effects of other gases are calculated as multiples of this value. In other words, a GWP calculation converts the emissions of non-CO_2 gases into CO_2 equivalents. Hydrofluorocarbons, perfluorocarbons, and sulfur compounds can be very stable and have long atmospheric lives, meaning they can stay in the earth's atmosphere, in some cases as long as several thousand years. A long atmospheric life allows a gas to build up over time. So, for example, hydrofluorocarbons have a GWP between 1,300 and 1,400.

The Focus on Carbon

The greenhouse gas that most concerns climate experts is human-made carbon dioxide (CO_2), often simply called carbon. This emphasis on carbon is because, over the past two decades, according to the EIA, about 75 percent of human-caused emissions came from burning fossil fuels, resulting in elevated carbon levels in Earth's atmosphere. For the year 2006 alone, the EIA calculated that 82 percent of greenhouse gas emissions in the United States came from energy-related carbon dioxide. According to the nonprofit group the Nature Conservancy, the United States generates 22 percent of the world's carbon emissions but represents only 5 percent of the world's population. Of U.S. carbon emissions, 20 percent is generated by individuals driving cars and trucks. The high rate of American contribution to carbon emissions was the crux of the controversy over the refusal of the administration of U.S. President George W. Bush to ratify the Kyoto Protocol, an international agreement that outlines cooperation to reduce the emission of greenhouse gases to counter global warming. Specifically, the protocol set binding targets for thirty-seven industrialized countries and the European Community in reducing their greenhouse gas emissions. Bush opted out of the treaty in 2001, explaining that implementation of the emissions restrictions would have damaged the American economy.

But at a December 2009 climate summit in Copenhagen, Denmark, U.S. President Barack Obama worked out a "meaningful and unprecedented agreement"[13] with the leaders of China, India, and South Africa in what U.S. officials called a "historic first step forward"[14] on climate change action. Through tense negotiations, developed and developing nations alike agreed to list national actions and commitments toward reducing greenhouse gas emissions. Although the Copenhagen conference set goals and outlined reporting mechanisms, the agreement was non-binding. President Obama, though pleased with the outcome, also acknowledged that more must be done to actually achieve significant reductions in global-warming pollution.

What Can Be Done?

How can human behavior be changed enough to make a difference? A good first step is to make the individual aware of his or her carbon footprint—the measurable amount of carbon that is released as a result of everyday human activities such as driving a car, eating food (some of which has been transported over substantial distances), traveling on airplanes, and heating or cooling a home. Armed with this knowledge, individuals can take action to reduce their own environmental impact. The concept echoes the Leave No Trace principles embraced by outdoor enthusiasts, the idea that the individual is accountable for how he or she in-

How Is a Carbon Footprint Calculated?

The inputs that calculators use to figure out a person's or a household's carbon footprint are:

- State of residence
- Number of people in the household
- Car model and number of miles driven yearly
- Number and length of airline flights yearly
- Average monthly electric bill
- Percent of household electricity that is derived from clean and renewable energy sources
- Average monthly natural gas, heating oil, and/or propane bill

Some calculators also ask general questions about how a home is heated, cooled, and lit; where the household buys food and the kinds of food choices that are made in the home; and how much recycling takes place in the household. These calculators, which take into account more daily habits, provide a better snapshot of a carbon footprint. One can be found at the Nature Conservancy's Web site, nature.org.

teracts with the environment in order to leave it as pristine as possible. Although humans cannot live on Earth without leaving some mark, if many individuals take steps to make a difference in their own impact, it will add up in the aggregate. Or, as Nobel laureate Archbishop Desmond Tutu observed, "Do your little bit of good where you are; it's those little bits of good put together that overwhelm the world."

Notes

1. International Panel on Climate Change, "Summary for Policymakers," *Climate Change 2007: The Physical Science Basis; Contribution of Working Group I to the Fourth Assessment Report of the Intergovernmental Panel on Climate Change*, ed. Susan Solomon et al. New York: Cambridge University Press, 2007. http://ipcc-wg1.ucar.edu.
2. IPCC, "Summary for Policymakers."
3. "The Nobel Peace Prize 2007," Nobelprize.org. www.nobelprize.org .
4. Natural Resources Defense Council, "Global Warming Puts the Arctic on Thin Ice: Answers to Questions About the Arctic's Shrinking Ice Cap and Its Global Significance," November 11, 2005. www.nrdc.org.
5. Planet Earth Online, "Pine Island Glacier May Disappear Within 100 Years," August 14, 2009. http://planetearth.nerc.ac.uk.
6. Planet Earth Online, "Pine Island Glacier May Disappear Within 100 Years."
7. Quoted in Gelu Sulugiuc, "Sea Levels Rising Faster than Expected," *Reuters*, March 10, 2009. www.reuters.com.
8. NASA, "Sea Ice May Be on Increase in Antarctic: A Phenomenon Due to a Lot of 'Hot Air'?" August 16, 2005. www.nasa.gov.
9. Quoted in "Scope," *Newsweek*, January 18, 2010, p. 7.
10. Michael Pidwirny, "The Carbon Cycle," *Fundamentals of Physical Geography*, 2nd ed., 2006. www.physicalgeography.net.
11. U.S. Energy Information Administration, "What Are Greenhouse Gases?" May 2008. www.eia.doe.gov.
12. U.S. Environmental Protection Agency, "High Global Warming Potential (GWP) Gases," March 25, 2010. www.epa.gov.
13. "Remarks by the President During Press Availability in Copenhagen," December 18, 2009. http://whitehouse.gov.
14. Quoted in Jason M. Brewslow, "Reports: Leaders Strike 'Meaningful Agreement' in Copenhagen," *PBS News Hour*, December 18, 2009. www.pbs.org.

CHAPTER 2

House and Garden

There are about 130 million homes in the United States and about 13 million in Canada, and these homes account for a substantial share of energy use—22 percent of the U.S. total in 2008 and 16 percent of the Canadian total in 2006 (the most recent statistics available). According to the U.S. Department of Energy (DOE), a typical U.S. household consumes about 11,000 kilowatt-hours (kWh) per year, costing an average of $1,034 annually. One kilowatt-hour, or kWh, equals 1,000 watt-hours (a watt-hour is a unit of energy equal to the power of one watt operating for one hour).

Heating, ventilation, and air conditioning (HVAC) systems use more energy than any other in-home system: According to the DOE, in a typical home, 43 percent of utility bills goes toward heating and cooling the home. The associated emissions are also substantial: These activities release 150 million tons of carbon dioxide into the atmosphere each year. If each individual household reduced energy consumption by only a small margin, the result would add up significantly. As Patrick Gonzalez, climate change scientist for the Nature Conservancy, remarked, "Each person can make a difference because one small positive act multiplied millions of times produces immense benefits."[1]

Home Energy Audit

The first step to saving energy is assessing a household's energy consumption through a home energy audit. Once the recom-

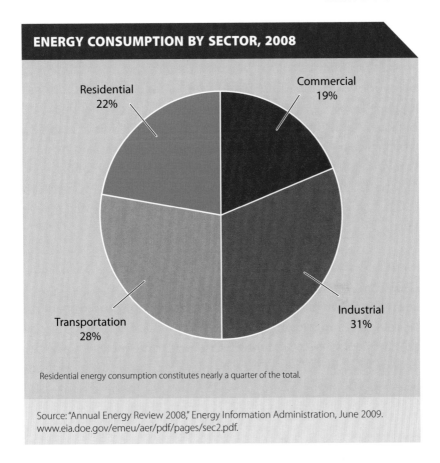

ENERGY CONSUMPTION BY SECTOR, 2008

Residential 22%

Commercial 19%

Industrial 31%

Transportation 28%

Residential energy consumption constitutes nearly a quarter of the total.

Source: "Annual Energy Review 2008," Energy Information Administration, June 2009. www.eia.doe.gov/emeu/aer/pdf/pages/sec2.pdf.

mendations of the audit are implemented, the result will be a more energy-efficient structure as well as lower utility bills and increased comfort in the home.

A do-it-yourself (DIY) audit can be conducted. Energy Star, a joint program of the U.S. Environmental Protection Agency and the U.S. Department of Energy, publishes a Home Energy Yardstick that requires only a short time to complete. Twelve months of utility bills are needed to supply accurate information. For comparing average utility bills to the average utility bill of an energy-efficient home in the same zip code, the DOE offers a Home Energy Saver tool (at http://hes.lbl.gov), described as the first Web-based home energy audit.

A professional home energy auditor can make specific recommendations for improving the efficiency of a home. Professional audits yield more detailed information and more recommendations than do DIY audits. According to Energy Star, thorough audits often use equipment such as blower doors, which measure the extent of leaks in the home's structure, and infrared cameras, which reveal hard-to-detect areas of air infiltration and missing insulation. Some utility companies offer free or discounted energy audits to their customers. Home Energy Rater information can be found at the Energy Star Web site by using the Home Partner Locator tool in the Home Performance section.

Increasing the Energy Efficiency of Existing Structures

There are many changes, small and large, that can be made to increase a home's energy efficiency. This chapter focuses on the building envelope (the home's structure) and mechanicals (the systems operating within the home, such as heating, ventila-

Solar panels convert electromagnetic radiation from the sun into usable energy for this house in Marshfield, Massachusetts. AP Images.

tion, cooling, and plumbing). (Energy savings in the home are discussed further in Chapter 3: Daily Living at Home.) To help motivate Americans to increase the energy efficiency of their homes, in 2009 the U.S. government began offering tax credits to consumers who made energy-saving changes to their homes, such as replacing exterior windows or doors. The DOE offers detailed information at its Web site. The American Council for an Energy-Efficient Economy (ACEEE), a nonprofit dedicated to advancing energy efficiency as a means of promoting economic prosperity, energy security, and environmental protection, also publishes an annual list of available tax incentives for increasing the energy efficiency of the home. The organization also provides a link on its site for consumers to check whether their local utility companies offer any rebates for upgrading home systems to energy-efficient models.

Heating and Cooling When new mechanicals are needed in the home, requiring an up-front investment as well as professional installation, it is important to consider the options. The ACEEE suggests that if a furnace or boiler is more than twenty years old it would be a good investment to replace it with a high-efficiency model. A replacement should also be considered if a home is equipped with any of the following:

- An old coal burner that was previously switched over to oil or gas

- An old gas furnace without electronic ignition: If it has a pilot light, it was probably installed prior to 1992 and has an efficiency of about 65 percent (the least efficient systems today are 80 percent)

- An old gas furnace without vent dampers or an induced draft fan; these devices limit the flow of heated air up the chimney when the heating system is off

If a furnace or boiler is between ten and twenty years old, and the household is experiencing high utility bills or interior climate discomfort, the ACEEE recommends hiring a highly qualified home-performance or heating contractor who can evaluate the existing system. Often it will be cost-effective to improve house insulation and air-tightness, repair or insulate ductwork, or tune up the system.

According to the DOE, similar considerations apply to cooling systems. If a home does not have a central air conditioning (AC) system, the DOE advises adding one as a more energy-efficient option than room air conditioners. In addition to being more efficient, central air conditioners are out of the way, quiet, and convenient to operate. The DOE reports that in an average air-conditioned home, air conditioning consumes more than 2,000 kilowatt-hours (kWh) of electricity per year, causing power plants to emit about 3,500 pounds (1,589 kilograms) of carbon dioxide (CO_2). Therefore, it is important that the AC unit is efficient and that the household minimizes its use. If an air conditioner is old, it may be possible to replace the compressor with a modern, high-efficiency unit. This service must be done by a heating and cooling contractor to ensure that the new compressor is properly matched to the unit. The DOE adds, however, that because there have been recent changes in refrigerants and air conditioning designs, it might be better to replace the entire system. Today's best air conditioners use 30 to 50 percent less energy to produce the same amount of cooling as air conditioners made in the mid-1970s. Even if an air conditioner is only ten years old, it is possible to save between 20 and 40 percent of household cooling energy costs by replacing it with a newer, more efficient model.

The DOE reports that proper sizing and installation are key elements in determining air conditioner efficiency. Too large a unit will not adequately remove humidity. Too small a unit will not be able to provide a comfortable temperature on the hottest days. Improper unit location, lack of insulation, and incorrect duct installation can greatly diminish efficiency. When buying an air conditioner, it is important to look for a high-efficiency model. Central air conditioners are rated according to their seasonal energy efficiency ratio (SEER). SEER indicates the relative amount of energy needed to provide a specific cooling output. Many older systems have SEER ratings of six or less. The minimum SEER allowed as of 2009 was thirteen. Consumers should look for the Energy Star label for central air conditioners with SEER ratings of thirteen or higher. The higher the SEER rating, the greater the savings will be in terms of energy and cost.

Because no two houses are alike, each home must be considered individually to identify the most appropriate, efficient, and cost-effective heating and cooling solutions. Finding a contractor whose focus is on high-efficiency systems is imperative. A skilled heating and cooling system technician with appropriate credentials (such as North American Technician Excellence training or Energy Star experience) should first perform a home evaluation and heat-loss calculation to determine proper sizing before making a recommendation.

Renewable Energy Sources

As of 2009 most homes in the United States continued to be heated by natural gas (53 percent) and electricity (30 percent). An estimated 10 percent of American homes were still heated by oil. But other energy sources were gaining ground. Renewable energy resources (such as wind, solar, and geothermal for the home) are abundant. These alternatives produce virtually no emissions or solid waste. The administration of U.S. President Barack Obama stated that "America can be the 21st century clean energy leader by harnessing the power of alternative and renewable energy."[2] Amid this atmosphere of energy awareness, heat pumps and solar panels have emerged as practical systems for home heating, ventilating, and air conditioning (HVAC).

High-Efficiency Heat Pumps Heat pump technology has been developed into a highly efficient system for transferring heat. The most common types of heat pumps are ones that draw heat from the air (air-source systems) or ones that draw heat from the ground (geothermal systems). The DOE compares the technology to that of the household refrigerator: A heat pump uses electricity to move heat from a cool space into a warm space, making the cool space cooler and the warm space warmer. According to the California Energy Commission's Consumer Energy Center, even cold air contains a great deal of heat; the temperature at which air no longer carries any heat is well below –200°F (–129°C). For people who live in climates with moderate heating and cooling needs, air-source heat pumps offer an energy-efficient alternative to furnaces and air conditioners. In winter months, an air-source heat pump will move heat from the cool outdoors into the home; during summer months, the same pump will move heat from inside the house into the warm outdoors. Because these pumps move heat rather than generate it, they can provide up to four times the amount of energy they consume. According to the DOE, if a home is heated with electricity, a heat pump can trim the amount of electricity used for heating by as much as 30 to 40 percent. For cooling, high-efficiency heat pumps dehumidify better than standard central air conditioners, resulting in less energy usage and more cooling comfort in summer months. The DOE adds that special air-source heat pumps can be installed even in homes without ducts or in homes that use radiant heat systems.

Geothermal pumps are an appropriate choice for houses in more extreme climates, where winter temperatures drop below –5°F (–20°C). In geothermal systems, the source of the warm or cool air is either the ground or water. Geothermal systems work on the same principle as air-source pumps, moving heat to improve comfort inside the home. A geothermal pump, though costly to install, has a low operating cost because it relies on relatively constant ground or water temperatures, temperatures that are warmer than the outside air during winter and cooler than the outside air during summer. Installation cost depends on lot size, soil, and home landscape. Although the number of households installing geothermal pumps is relatively low, the system is becoming more popular. The U.S. Energy Information Administration (EIA) reported that in 2008 total shipments of geothermal heat pumps surged more than 40 percent (to 121,243 units) compared to the year before. The EIA credited increased demand to consumer concerns over the rising cost of energy and tighter budgets, which prompted homeowners to seek more efficient ways to heat and cool their homes. Also fueling the growth was the Emergency Economic Stabilization Act of 2009, which provides long-term tax incentives to encourage the use of renewable energy technologies, including geothermal heat pumps for homes. High-efficiency heat pumps not only save energy, they prevent pollution, reduce greenhouse gas emissions, and reduce a household's carbon footprint.

Solar Energy Electromagnetic radiation from the sun can be captured and converted into useful forms of energy in the home, for space heating, water heating, and electricity. Sunlight is the world's most reliable source of energy and the most copious; it is the most inexhaustible, renewable source of energy known, "providing more energy in 1 hour to the earth than all of the energy consumed by humans in an entire year."[3] Although there are some do-it-yourself ideas for capturing the sun's energy for residential applications, contacting a qualified solar energy contractor is advised. The practical use of solar energy systems depends on several factors, including location, area weather, and the home site.

Solar power is converted to energy primarily through the placement of photovoltaic cells, also called solar cells, under direct sunlight; when the sun's rays hit the cells, a chemical reaction is initiated, creating an electric current.

Two key terms to understand in solar energy are passive and active. Passive solar energy uses the sun's radiation for practical purposes (space heating and water heating) with little or no use of other energy sources. Passive solar depends entirely on the structure's site and design. According to the DOE, passive solar building design, also called climatic design, uses a structure's windows, walls, and floors to collect, store, and distribute the sun's heat in the winter and reject solar heat in the summer. It can also maximize the use of sunlight for interior illumination. Day-lighting takes advantage of natural sunlight, through well-placed windows and specialized floor plans, to brighten a building's interior.

Incorporating solar design elements into homes can reduce heating bills by as much as 50 percent.

Passive solar design has several advantages: It is highly energy efficient, reducing a structure's energy demands for lighting, winter heating, and summer cooling; it reduces demand for fossil fuel; it is nonpolluting and will not contribute to greenhouse gas emissions; and it saves money because energy from the sun is free. A design that is strictly passive captures the sun's energy without investments in mechanical and electrical devices such as pumps, fans, or electrical controls. According to the DOE, incorporating solar design elements into homes can reduce heating bills by as much as 50 percent. The department adds that a "well-designed and built passive solar building does not have to sacrifice aesthetics either. It can be as attractive as conventionally designed buildings and still save energy and money."[4]

Before a structure that incorporates passive solar design is built, certain advantages and disadvantages should be considered. Passive solar design costs more than conventional building design, but the up-front investment pays for itself over time because of savings in energy expenses. Construction costs may run higher (especially in certain regions) than conventional construction costs; again, it is expected that long-term savings would offset these expenses. It is imperative that the right kind of glass is chosen for each side of the building: different window glazings (invisible glass coatings) will work to reduce solar gain or to reduce heat loss. The type of glazing that is needed can be determined by qualified contractors. The design must also account for interior placement of televisions and computer screens to minimize glare. Finally, the climate must be carefully considered so that day-lighting does not overburden the air-conditioning load, offsetting any savings in energy and cost. Despite these concerns, the DOE notes that passive solar buildings have been constructed as far north as Maine and as far south as Florida.

Active solar heating systems feature panels, located on rooftops or southern exposures, that absorb and collect the sun's radiation; it, in turn, warms air or fluid (water or an antifreeze solution); the warmed air or fluid is then distributed by electric pumps or fans to heat an interior space. Most active systems are able to store energy so that a home can be heated when the sun is not shining—at night or on a cloudy day. Air-based systems may also supply heat to a hot-water system, replacing a conventional water heater.

The pros of an active solar system are that sun provides an endless source of clean and renewable energy; the energy system's price is set (once the system is installed, it uses sunlight, which is free); and state and federal governments were, as of 2010, offering tax incentives to consumers who switched to solar. The cons of these systems are that they are expensive to install (although that up-front cost is expected to be recouped over the first several years of the system's life) and that certain places on earth do not receive enough sunlight to make a solar energy system viable. Most energy experts conclude that the pros of solar energy outweigh the cons.

Wind Power Humans have used the wind's energy for hundreds of years; long before the industrial revolution, windmills were used to pump water or process grain, and the wind's power propelled boats. According to the American Wind Energy Association (AWEA), "wind energy is a converted form of solar energy. The sun's radiation heats different parts of the earth at different rates—most notably during the day and night, but also when different surfaces (for example, water and land) absorb or reflect at different rates. This in turn causes portions of the atmosphere to warm differently. Hot air rises, reducing the atmospheric pressure at the earth's surface, and cooler air is drawn in to replace it. The result is wind." The AWEA goes on to explain that "air has mass, and when it is in motion, it contains the energy of that motion (kinetic energy). Some portion of that energy can be converted into other forms—mechanical force or electricity—that we can use to perform work."[5]

Today's wind-power technology is focused on turbines that generate electricity or pump water. Small wind energy systems, installed for residential purposes, are limited to buildings situated on at least one acre of land, to areas where municipal codes allow the erection and operation of a turbine or turbines, and to regions where there is enough wind to turn the rotor blades. Homeowners whose situations satisfy these requirements should seek a qualified installer.

Even some urban and suburban homeowners can take advantage of modern wind technology by purchasing their electricity from a wind power plant—a plant that distributes electricity generated by wind farms. These plants carry many advantages, including serving as backup to existing conventional power sources, which are not 100 percent reliable. According to the National Renewable Energy Lab (NREL), "When wind is added to a utility system, no new backup is required to maintain system reliability."[6] The use of wind power is on the rise. In 2007, 35 percent of all new generation capacity added to the electric grid in the United States was from wind power projects. The AWEA explains that electric utilities are "increasingly adding wind power to their power supply portfolios, as a clean, inexhaustible, and domestic source of electric generation."[7]

Investing in utility companies that emphasize wind power, even if it is for strictly commercial applications, is also an option for the individual. According to the AWEA, there were 31,109 wind energy projects in the United States as of mid-2009 and another 5,567 under construction. The DOE aims to boost wind energy's contribution to the U.S. electrical supply, increasing it to 20 percent of the whole by 2030. Identifying and researching publicly owned companies with wind energy interests are the first steps investors should take.

Add-On Solutions

When evaluating the energy efficiency of a home, it is important to look beyond the central systems. In many cases, a home's mechanicals will work more efficiently with some help.

Keeping Humidity Under Control A key component of heating and cooling is controlling interior humidity levels—the amount of water vapor in the air. Dry air feels cooler to the skin than moist air; keeping a home less humid in summer months and more humid in winter months ensures a higher comfort level for the household and should reduce energy costs. The energy savings is achieved through shorter run times for air conditioners and furnaces or heaters. If the humidity level is adjusted to the appropriate setting for the season, the thermostat can be turned higher in summer and lower in winter without sacrificing comfort. Humidifiers and dehumidifiers can be added to existing systems. Proper ventilation of areas that create moisture, such as bathrooms, is a key component to controlling interior humidity levels. Do-it-yourself guides to solving interior humidity problems can be researched online; local heating, ventilation, and air-conditioning contractors can install whole-house humidifiers and dehumidifiers.

Whole-House Ventilation Fans installed in attics or on roofs draw warm air out of the house in summer months, reducing the need for air conditioning. Whole-house fans also help bring fresh air into the home. Again, the energy savings is in reduced run times for air-conditioning units.

Wood-Burning Fires Most fireplaces and older wood stoves are big polluters. Burning wood creates numerous byproducts, including carbon dioxide (CO_2), carbon monoxide, nitrogen, sulfur dioxide, and methane. Not only are these chemicals bad for the environment, they are bad for human health. But proponents argue that because the fuel source is sustainable through the planting of more trees, wood burning can be an efficient and, given the right equipment, an environmentally friendly way to heat a home.

Most home fireplaces are inefficient at burning wood and therefore produce an inordinate amount of emissions. With this in mind, in 2009 the Obama administration announced tax incentives for Americans who purchase qualifying (efficient) modern wood-burning stoves or fireplace inserts (wood stoves that have been converted to fit in existing fireplace openings). Although this push to convert old fireplaces and replace outdated wood stoves should have the effect of reducing U.S. emissions from wood burning, opponents argue that the best way to reduce greenhouse gases is to not cut down trees in the first place. Indeed, deforestation is a major contributor to global warming.

Air Leakage

A critical component of a home's energy efficiency is air leakage or drafts. Locating and fixing air leaks through proper weatherization increases energy efficiency up to 10 percent per year, according to the DOE. Once leaks are fixed, the home will feel more comfortable. Electrical outlets, switch plates, window frames, baseboards, door frames, fireplace dampers, attic hatches, wall- or window-mounted air conditioners, gaps at the edges of floors and at the junctures of walls and ceilings, pipes, wires, and mail slots should be checked. Air ducts should be checked for leaks at their seams. If air leaks are found, they can be fixed with caulk, foam, and other weatherproofing materials. Insulating curtains or blinds reduce draftiness at old windows, though replacing the window is the better option in the long term.

The U.S. government offers help through a Weatherization and Intergovernmental Program, which provides consumers with information on cost, performance, and financing of energy efficiency and renewable energy projects. Through the Weatherization Assistance Program, the DOE delivers weatherization services to low-income households in every county in the nation and on Native American tribal lands. Through a network of partnerships with more than 970 local weatherization agencies, the program improves the energy efficiency of more than one hundred thousand low-income dwellings a year.

Home Insulation Making sure there is enough insulation in the walls, foundation, and roof (anywhere there is a barrier between the home and the outside) is one of the best ways to make a home energy efficient. The type and amount of insulation depends on regional climate. The DOE publishes regularly updated standards and information on insulation at its energysavers.gov Web site. An important term to keep in mind when investigating insulation is the R-value. It indicates an insulating material's resistance to heat flow: the higher the R-value, the greater the insulating effectiveness. Because warm air rises, insulating an attic is a good defense against heat loss. Fiberglass (loose-fill or batting) is the most common insulator. Other insulating materials include cellulose (shredded newspaper), recycled denim, and wool. When considering basement insulation, seeking the help of a qualified contractor is advised, because many insulating materials will lose effectiveness if they get wet.

Replacement Windows and Doors About one third of a home's total heat loss occurs through windows and doors, according to the American Council for an Energy-Efficient Economy. Replacements should be considered if any of the following applies: wood is rotted or damaged, glass is cracked, putty is missing, a vinyl or aluminum frame is damaged, sashes do not fit well, or window or door will not lock. Replacement windows should be Energy Star–certified, air-tight, and glazed with a low-e (low emissivity) coating to reduce solar heat gain. In addition, windows should have multiple layers of glazing (double glazing insulates almost twice as well as single glazing) as well as low-conductivity gas fill (such as argon) to reduce heat loss. It is recommended that windows be installed by an experienced contractor according to manufacturer specifications. To help consumers compare windows, the National Fenestration Rating Council puts its label on Energy Star–qualified windows and doors. This label provides performance information in the following categories:

- *U-factor* This number measures how well a product prevents heat from escaping. U-factor ratings generally fall between 0.20 and 1.20. The lower the U-factor, the greater a window's resistance to heat flow and the better its insulating value.

- *Solar heat gain coefficient (SHGC)* Expressed as a number between 0 and 1, this measures how well a product blocks heat caused by sunlight. The lower a window's solar heat gain coefficient, the less solar heat it transmits into the house.

- *Visible transmittance* Measured on a scale of 0 to 1, this number describes the amount of sunlight that can pass through a window. The higher the number, the more light (not energy) can pass through.

- *Air leakage (AL)* Heat loss and gain occur by infiltration through cracks in the window assembly. The lower the AL, the less air will pass through cracks in the window assembly.

- *Condensation resistance* Measured on a scale of 0 to 100, this number describes a window's ability to resist condensation on the interior surface of the window. The higher the rating, the better the product will resist condensation. This rating cannot predict condensation; it compares the potential of various products for condensation formation.

Green Building

The U.S. Environmental Protection Agency (EPA) defines green building as "the practice of creating structures and using processes that are environmentally responsible and resource-efficient throughout a building's life-cycle from siting to design, construction, operation, maintenance, renovation and deconstruction."[8] The EPA explains that the practice expands and complements the classical building design concerns of economy, utility, durability, and comfort. The principles of green building, also known as sustainable or high-performance building, include resource efficiency and the use of recycled materials or environmentally friendly materials. Components of a green home would include several or all of the following:

- A site selected with passive solar energy in mind—taking advantage of natural sunlight and shade to reduce heating, cooling, and lighting usage
- Thermal windows
- Radiant heat
- On-demand water heater
- Cellulose (recycled newspaper) or recycled denim insulation
- Finished concrete and bamboo floors
- Dual-flush toilets
- No-VOC (volatile organic compounds) paint
- Energy Star appliances
- Smart-home technology (which allows homeowners to control lighting and temperature remotely)

Leading organizations have developed guidelines for green building. The U.S. Green Building Council, a Washington, D.C.–based nonprofit, established the LEED (Leadership in Energy and Environmental Design) Green Building Rating System to encourage and accelerate global adoption of sustainable green building and development practices through these universally

Impact of Green Building

Energy Star, a joint program of the U.S. Environmental Protection Agency and the U.S. Department of Energy, provides one snapshot of the impact of home energy efficiency. According to program data, 109,857 homes built in 2008 were Energy Star–qualified. These homes were the equivalent of the following:

- Eliminating emissions from 53,830 vehicles
- Saving 325,616,148 pounds (147,829,731 kilograms) of coal
- Planting 88,984 acres (36,012 hectares) of trees
- Saving the environment 638,598,741 pounds (289,923,828 kilograms) of CO_2

All figures are based on national averages.

understood and accepted tools and performance criteria. In addition, the National Association of Home Builders (NAHB) publishes annual standards for green building, saying it is not a trend but the future of home building. With the passage of the American Recovery and Reinvestment Act in 2009, funds were made available by the government to encourage green building; information can be found at the EPA Web site.

Yards and Gardens

Backyard conservation falls into three categories: (1) saving energy by reducing the use of fossil fuel– or electric-powered lawn and garden equipment; (2) reducing water consumption; and (3) eliminating or reducing the application of synthetic chemicals—fertilizers, herbicides, pesticides. To go green in the yard or garden, any or all of the following principles should be used.

Minimizing Turf As pundits have noted, there is no such thing as a green lawn. In other words, though the turf may be green in color, it cannot be green environmentally because maintaining a lawn produces greenhouse gases. Expanses of turf require routine maintenance including regular cutting, often with a gasoline-powered mower. Additionally, many people treat lawns with either broad or spot applications of chemicals to encourage growth, control weeds, and ward off insects that may damage turf. Synthetic chemicals require energy to produce, and their runoff is harmful to humans and other animals as well as to the environment. The best practice is to reduce turf expanses to the minimum that is needed for recreation and devote the balance of the home landscape to gardens that are planted with native species.

Planting Smart Choosing plants that are native to the region reduces the amount of help or coaxing plants need in order to thrive. Native species are well-adapted to local climates, including precipitation levels.

Xeriscaping Also called zeroscaping, this practice emphasizes seven basic principles that save water:

1. Planning and design
2. Soil analysis (once a soil's composition is understood, it can be safely amended to encourage the growth of native plants)
3. Practical turf areas (expanses of turf that are appropriately sized to the practical needs of the household)
4. Appropriate plant selection (plants that are native to the region)
5. Efficient irrigation
6. Use of mulches
7. Appropriate maintenance (trimming, pruning, and dividing plants as necessary)

The xeriscaping concept was developed as a landscaping solution for arid climates, but its basic principles translate to any region and reduce yard maintenance.

Planting Trees to Shade the House in Summer Months According to the Nature Conservancy, a strategically planted shade tree can reduce the energy required to run a home's air conditioner, saving 200 to 2,000 pounds (90 to 900 kilograms) of carbon over the tree's lifetime.

Organic Practices Fertilizing, controlling weeds, and eliminating pests can be accomplished using organic methods. They include diverse plant selection, companion planting (to divert pests), raised garden beds, composting and other natural soil-building practices, mulching to keep down weeds, encouraging beneficial insects and animals, and using pheromone traps and insecticidal soap sprays before resorting to applications of organic pesticides. A compound's being labeled organic does not mean it is safe; checking with a local or regional gardening authority is advised.

Composting The nutrients in gardening soil can be boosted through composting, which is explored in greater detail in Chapter 3: Daily Living at Home.

Rain Barrels Capturing rainfall and using that water for as-needed irrigation cuts down on household water demand. As the transport of water requires energy (and the farther it is transported, the more energy is required), reducing water consumption is an energy-saving practice.

Hand Tools Using lawn and garden tools that are human-powered will reduce the use of gasoline and electricity in lawn and shrub maintenance. Muscle power fuels these old-fashioned devices, including motorless push mowers with rotating blades, brooms and rakes (instead of blowers), and hedge shears.

More information on planning a landscape that suits the local environment, thereby demanding fewer resources over the long term, can be found at regional botanical gardens, landscape centers, and agricultural extensions of colleges and universities.

Notes

1. Quoted in "Climate Change: What You Can Do," *Nature Conservancy*, February 4, 2010. www.nature.org.
2. "Organizing on the Issues: New Energy," *Organizing for America*, February 4, 2010. www.barackobama.com.
3. Nathan S. Lewis and Daniel G. Nocera, "Powering the Planet: Chemical Challenges in Solar Energy Utilization," *Proceedings of the National Academy of Sciences of the United States of America*, August 11, 2006. http://www.pnas.org.
4. U.S. Department of Energy, "Passive Solar Home Design," February 24, 2009. www.energysavers.gov.
5. American Wind Energy Association, "Wind Web Tutorial," February 4, 2010. www.awea.org/faq.
6. National Renewable Energy Laboratory, "Frequently Asked Questions About Systems Integration," November 20, 2008. www.nrel.gov.
7. American Wind Energy Association, "Utilities and Wind Power," February 4, 2010. www.awea.org.
8. U.S. Environmental Protection Agency, "Green Building: Basic Information," October 21, 2009. www.epa.gov.

CHAPTER 3

Daily Living at Home

There are many ways to decrease household energy use on a daily basis, thereby curbing emissions of greenhouse gases. Most of these reductions can be accomplished without a great deal of trouble or expense, and some are simply a matter of changing habits. Furthermore, even the smallest reductions in energy use come with a bonus—out-of-pocket savings. For example, according to the nonprofit American Council for an Energy-Efficient Economy (ACEEE), a typical U.S. household would save about 10 percent on its annual heating bill by lowering the thermostat from 70°F to 65°F (from 21°C to 18°C) for at least eight hours a day in winter months. The more households that take such steps as these, the greater the reduction of greenhouse gases in the atmosphere.

Heating and Cooling the Home

If a heating and cooling system is out of date and a drain on energy, it should be replaced, as discussed in the previous chapter. But many energy gains can be made through no-cost or low-cost measures. If the following steps are taken, the home can remain comfortable to the inhabitants while still saving energy.

Adjusting the Thermostat One of the easiest things to change is home temperature, and in this category the greenhouse gas reductions add up quickly. In the United States, almost half of

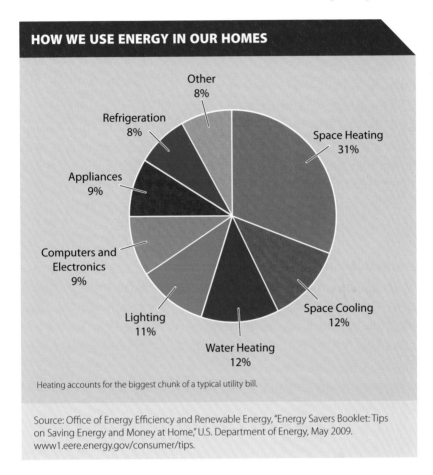

HOW WE USE ENERGY IN OUR HOMES

Other
8%

Refrigeration
8%

Space Heating
31%

Appliances
9%

Computers and
Electronics
9%

Lighting
11%

Space Cooling
12%

Water Heating
12%

Heating accounts for the biggest chunk of a typical utility bill.

Source: Office of Energy Efficiency and Renewable Energy, "Energy Savers Booklet: Tips on Saving Energy and Money at Home," U.S. Department of Energy, May 2009. www1.eere.energy.gov/consumer/tips.

home energy use (43 percent) is attributable to heating and cooling. By extension, the carbon output generated by home heating and cooling is substantial. Simply by lowering the furnace temperature 2°F (about 1°C) in winter months and raising the air conditioning temperature 2°F in summer months, a typical household could save about 2,000 pounds (900 kilograms) a year of CO_2 emissions. A rule of thumb is that for every degree of change in the right direction, about 500 pounds of carbon emissions are cut per year. These figures are generalized; results vary depending on regional climate and other contributing factors. A home energy audit, as discussed in greater detail in Chapter 2: House and Garden, can help homeowners assess their situation.

Again, there are cost savings. According to the ACEEE, a household will save 2 percent on the heating bill for every 1°F (.5°C) that the thermostat is lowered for at least eight hours a day. The ACEEE also refutes the common notion that it takes more energy to bring a home back to a desired temperature than it would to leave the home at the optimum temperature all day. In short, moving the thermostat up in summer months and down in winter months will conserve energy and cut emissions as well as heating and cooling bills.

Programmable Thermostats An efficient way to manage household temperature is with a programmable thermostat. This low-cost device keeps air temperatures constant and allows temperature adjustments to be programmed based on household schedules. When no one is home, the furnace or air conditioner need not work as hard to moderate air temperature. If different temperatures are desired upon rising or at bedtime, they can be programmed as well.

Replacing or cleaning a dirty air filter can save a household 350 pounds of CO_2 emissions each year.

Air Filters The filters on furnaces and air conditioners need to be changed regularly. A heating or cooling unit must work harder to move air through filters that are clogged with dirt. The Pew Center on Global Climate Change calculates that replacing or cleaning a dirty air filter can save a household 350 pounds of CO_2 emissions each year.

Most furnace recommendations call for changing the air filter monthly; checking owner's manuals is advised. The best method is to stock up on filters seasonally and set a regular day of the month (such as the first or the last) on which the filter is changed. Window air conditioning units have filters that can be rinsed with water, allowed to air dry, and then replaced in the unit. Experts also recommend that old foam filters be replaced with plastic electrostatic mesh filters, which work better to trap particles that reduce unit performance. The plastic electrostatic material can be purchased in kits in hardware and home improvement stores.

Ventilation Ceiling fans can help keep a house feeling warmer in winter and cooler in summer, reducing dependency on heaters and air conditioners. Fans should rotate clockwise (pulling cool air up) in the winter and counterclockwise (pulling warm air up) in the summer. A switch on the base of the fan toggles between the two rotations.

Kitchen, bath, and other exhaust fans should be turned off within twenty minutes after cooking or bathing. If it is time to replace fans, the U.S. Department of Energy (DOE) recommends high-efficiency, low-noise models.

To keep central heating and air conditioning systems running at peak performance, vents and registers should be clean and dust-free, as well as unobstructed by household objects. The same is true for baseboard heaters and radiators.

Solar Gain and Loss Controlling the flow of natural light into the home is a component of heating and cooling. Window coverings can be more than decorative. Ones that function well can be closed against the summer sun, keeping heat out of the home and causing air conditioners to run less. Drapes, curtains, and blinds, if kept open during moderate winter days, will allow sunlight into the home and boost solar warming. In winter, window treatments that are closed at night will reduce chill from cold windows.

Lighting
Lighting inside and outside the home is important for the safety and comfort of the dwellers, for productivity in work, and for en-

ergetic play. Smart habits regarding electricity use and new technologies can curb energy consumption while keeping a home properly lit inside and out.

The DOE urges consumers to look for the Energy Star label on new lamp fixtures: Energy Star–qualified fluorescent or LED (light-emitting diode) fixtures use 75 percent less energy than incandescent fixtures. Although LED technology is still emerging and is more expensive than either fluorescent or incandescent, it promises advantages including a substantially longer life, longer warranties, instant "on" (as opposed to fluorescents, which may

If a CFL or Other Fluorescent Bulb Breaks

The U.S. Environmental Protection Agency advises the following:

Air out the room
1. Have people and pets leave the room, and do not let anyone walk through the breakage area on the way out.
2. Open a window and leave the room for at least fifteen minutes.
3. Shut off the central forced-air heating or air conditioning system if there is one.

Clean hard surfaces, such as wood and tile
1. Carefully scoop up glass pieces and powder using stiff paper or cardboard; place them in a glass jar with a metal lid (such as a canning jar) or in a sealed plastic bag.
2. Using sticky tape, such as duct tape, pick up any remaining small glass fragments and powder.
3. Wipe the area clean with damp paper towels or disposable wet wipes. Place towels in a glass jar or plastic bag.
4. Do not use a vacuum or broom to clean up the broken bulb on hard surfaces.

take up to three minutes to reach 80 percent brightness), and cooler running temperatures.

The DOE also suggests consumers plan task lighting rather than whole-room lighting, to focus artificial light where it is needed. LED fixtures are particularly useful for task lighting—for desks, under kitchen cabinets, under shelves, for recessed ceiling lights, and as wall-mounted porch lights, outdoor step lights, and outdoor pathway lights.

Dimming the lights is another energy saver. If lights must be on, it is possible they do not need to burn their brightest.

Clean carpeting or rugs

1. Follow steps 1 and 2 for cleaning hard surfaces.
2. After all visible materials are removed, vacuum the area where the bulb was broken.
3. Remove the vacuum bag or empty and wipe the canister, and put the bag or vacuum debris in a sealed plastic bag.

Dispose of cleanup materials

1. Check with local or state government about disposal requirements in the area. Some states do not allow such trash disposal. Instead, they require that broken and unbroken mercury-containing bulbs be taken to a local recycling center.
2. If allowed, immediately place all cleanup materials outdoors in a trash container or protected area for the next normal trash pickup.
3. Wash hands after disposing of the jars or plastic bags containing cleanup materials.

Air the room during and after vacuuming in future cleaning of carpeting or rug

1. The next several times the vacuum is run, shut off the central forced-air heating or air conditioning system and open a window before vacuuming.
2. Keep the central heating or air conditioning system shut off and a window open for at least fifteen minutes after vacuuming is completed.

Installing dimmer switches is an inexpensive solution that is likely to save energy and money.

Another important consideration in interior lighting is color palette. Decorating techniques can reduce the need for artificial lighting. Light-colored curtains allow more sunlight into a room than do dark-colored ones. Decorating with light colors, on walls as well as on furnishings, helps brighten a room.

Compact Fluorescent Bulbs The relatively new compact fluorescent bulbs (CFLs) offer substantial savings in energy consumption. A CFL uses 60 percent less energy than a standard incandescent bulb. According to the Pew Center on Global Climate Change, if every family in the United States switched to CFLs, Americans could reduce their CO_2 output by more than 90 billion pounds (41 billion kilograms) per year.

The DOE reports that exterior lighting is one of the best places to use CFLs because of their long life. But in cold climates, lamp fixtures must be fitted with a cold-weather ballast as standard CFLs may not work well below 40°F (4.4°C).

CFLs perform especially well in comparison to halogen bulbs, which are found in some standing lamps, or torchieres. Compact fluorescent torchieres use 60 to 80 percent less energy than their halogen counterparts, and they can produce more light measured in lumens. CFLs also do not get as hot as halogens, which can be a fire risk because of the high temperature of the bulb.

For nightlights, four-watt mini-fluorescent or electroluminescent bulbs are more efficient than incandescent bulbs. In addition to saving energy, these bulbs burn more coolly than incandescents and remain cooler to the touch.

A word of caution: Because a CFL contains a very small amount of mercury (about 5 milligrams), it must be disposed of properly after use. The mercury content is minuscule and does not pose a health concern, as long as the used bulbs are disposed of according to recommended guidelines. Many hardware and home goods stores have drop boxes to collect used CFLs from their customers. Carefully recycling CFLs prevents the release of mercury into the environment and, according to the U.S. Environmental Protection Agency (EPA), allows for the reuse of glass, metals, and other materials that make up fluorescent lights.

Turning Off Lights When Not in Use Thrifty consumers practice energy conservation by following one simple rule: Turn off the lights when leaving a room. Dousing the lights when they are not in use can quickly add up to savings—of energy, emissions, and money. It may also be efficient to put household lights on timers, so they do not burn when no one is home, yet a lamp is lighting the way when residents return. Timers are inexpensive and easy to set up. Motion sensors can also be installed to similarly regulate lighting.

Outside Lighting For outdoor lighting, fixtures powered by photovoltaic (PV) cells, which convert solar energy to electricity, can provide practical footpath lighting in many, but not all, climates; there must be enough sunlight each day to fully charge the cells. Motion sensors turn lights on as they are needed and off when they are not, which, for most households, will cut energy use over the long term. Sensors that monitor daylight are also an option. They can be installed as plug-in units or hardwired by a licensed electrician into an existing exterior lighting fixture. These sensors activate outside lights at dusk and deactivate them at dawn, which may reduce energy use.

Outside lamps that are powered by natural gas are a sizeable energy drain. According to the DOE, just eight such lamps burning year-round use as much natural gas as it takes to heat an average-size home during an entire winter. Replacing these fixtures with electric-powered lamps or photocell-powered lamps is advised.

Monitoring Energy Use

Studies have shown that the more a person understands his or her household energy use in real time (or near real time), the more that can be done to reduce it. Emerging technologies provide consumers with information about their energy use. A smart meter shows consumption in more detail than a conventional meter, allowing the consumer to view hourly electric and daily gas energy usage data. In October 2009, the U.S. government announced $3.4 billion in grants to help pay for 18 million (roughly 13 percent of electricity meters nationwide) smart meters. The grants, which were to be awarded to utilities and related companies (which could then offer them to consumers), had the dual purpose of stimulating the economy and reducing long-term energy use nationwide. Additionally, homes equipped with smart meters can use Google's PowerMeter, a free electricity usage monitoring tool that provides information on iGoogle (a personalized Google Web page), delivering energy data to the desktop.

Working with Utility Companies to Reduce Energy Use

Most large utilities companies have implemented elective programs that allow customers to limit their energy use at certain times or under certain conditions. These programs include load guards and air conditioner cycling.

With a load guard option, consumers agree that the power company will cycle off their air conditioner during times of peak use. For example, in 2009, Chicago area provider ComEd promoted its Load Guard program as an "innovative set-and-forget feature that is designed to automatically cycle a participant's central air conditioning unit off and on during high-priced summer days."[1] Participants in this program were able to select a target price—either ten cents or fourteen cents per kilowatt-hour—that, once hit, would switch their central air conditioner into a conservation mode for a two-hour period (energy prices rise with demand, so as energy use rises, the price per kilowatt-hour also rises). Many participants reported they did not notice a discernible change in their comfort level due to the temporary powering down of the AC unit.

Homeowners who have central air conditioning can elect to have the power company install a switch on the unit, allowing the company to cycle the compressor on and off during high-demand summer days. In addition to having the air conditioning run less often, consumers may also receive a credit from the power company on their summer bills.

Small Electronics

Most households are equipped with a variety of small electrical devices such as cell phones, handheld music players (iPods), digital cameras, and cordless tools. But these small devices pose a big energy drain. According to the Pew Center on Climate Change, in the average home 75 percent of the electricity used to power home electronics is consumed while the products are in standby mode. Furthermore, the high-tech life comes with a big price tag. According to the DOE, electronics accounted for 15 percent of the average household's annual energy bill in 2008, whereas it was only 7 percent in 2001. Electronics should be unplugged at the power point when not in use or once they have been fully charged. The same is true of charging stations—they should be turned off or unplugged when not in use.

Larger home electronics such as computers, printers, televisions, home theater equipment, game systems, and stereos also cause an energy drain. According to data cited by the National Resources Defense Council (NRDC), even when these products are off, they continue to consume energy in standby mode—as much as the equivalent of continuously running a 75-watt or 100-watt light bulb. These electronics should be powered off when they are not in use. Additionally, owner's manuals for computers include information about power settings that can be adjusted by the user, allowing the computer to go into standby mode or turn itself off.

Power strips allow several devices to be turned off with one switch. Because power strips have become more energy efficient in recent years, old ones should be replaced. The newest innovation in this area is the smart power strip, which knows that when the television is turned off, it should turn off all the peripheral equipment as well. While these gadgets can cost around $100, they could also save consumers money over the long term by curbing energy use in electronic-intense corners of the home such as the entertainment center.

The Pew Center also reports that the energy that keeps display clocks lit and memory chips working accounts for 5 percent of total domestic energy consumption and spews 18 million tons of carbon into the atmosphere every year. Looking around each room in the home is likely to reveal small electronic devices that are not used regularly and should be unplugged. Hair dryers, extra clocks, idle printers, and small kitchen appliances (such as toaster ovens, food processors, and mixers) fall into this category. These devices may seem to have very small electricity uses, but it is important to consider the effect of many or even all households unplugging idle electronics. The NRDC, EPA, and DOE are among the many agencies and organizations encouraging consumers to unplug.

Appliances

Large household appliances also drain the earth's energy sources and inordinately contribute to greenhouse gas emissions. Washers, dryers, dishwashers, refrigerators, stoves, microwaves, and ovens that are more than 15 years old are energy and money wasters and should be replaced with new ones that bear the Energy Star logo. Front-loading, high-efficiency washers and dryers save energy and water as well as money. The cost of replacing old appliances is likely to be offset through future energy savings, based on the improved performance of the new appliance. Many utility companies will pick up old appliances for free.

According to the DOE, "When you're shopping for appliances, think of two price tags. The first one covers the purchase price—think of it as a down payment. The second price tag is the cost of operating the appliance during its lifetime. You'll be paying on that second price tag every month with your utility bill for the next 10 to 20 years, depending on the appliance. Refrigerators last an average of 14 years; clothes washers about 11 years; dishwashers about 10 years; and room air conditioners last 9 years."[2] The Energy Star Web site (www.energystar.gov) contains regularly updated product information and consumer guides for selecting appliances that consume less of the earth's resources.

Using appliances wisely and reducing their use are also key strategies in saving energy and cutting greenhouse gas emissions. Government and environmental organizations are unanimous in these recommendations:

- Dishwashers and clothes washers should be run only when fully loaded

- Clothes should be washed in cooler temperatures whenever possible (specially formulated detergents will clean any color of clothing using cold water only)

- Air-drying clothes, on lines or racks, is preferable to running the dryer

- Cooking with a microwave is more efficient than cooking with a standard oven

Keeping Refrigerators Running Efficiently To keep foods properly cooled and save energy, these tips should be followed:

- Manufacturers' recommendations for cleaning refrigerator coils should be followed to maximize cooling and prevent the unit from working harder than it needs to.

- Reducing how many times a day the refrigerator is opened saves energy: opening the door lets cold air out and warm air in; also, doors should always be completely closed after use.

- Refrigerators should be regularly purged of out-of-date foods to avoid unnecessary cooling of products that can no longer be consumed and to allow for maximal organization inside the refrigerator; good organization allows all household members to readily find what they are looking for and reduces the time the refrigerator door stands open.

- Thermostats should be set to 37 to 40°F (3 to 4°C) for refrigerators and 0 to 5°F (–17 to –15°C) for freezers; for refrigerators that do not display temperature, appliance thermometers are available at hardware stores and online retailers.

- Extra refrigerators that are not kept three-quarters full at all times should be unplugged and their contents moved to the main refrigerator; the three-quarters mark is the mass necessary to maintain steady internal temperatures.

Using Ovens and Ranges Efficiently Cooks and bakers who want to keep energy use under control should follow these tips:

- On electric stoves, pan size should be matched to burner size for efficient heating.

- Because electric burners remain hot even after being deactivated, they can be shut off a few minutes before the end of cook time without losing heat to the pot or pan.

- On gas stoves, flames should not reach around or up the sides of the pot.

- Judiciously preheating ovens is advised: Once the oven has reached the desired temperature, the food should be promptly put in and the timer set to avoid wasting energy.

Outdoor Grilling

A favorite summer activity, charcoal grilling, has come under scrutiny for the high quantity of greenhouse gases it produces. In May 2009 British researcher and environmental consultant Eric Johnson published an article in *Environmental Impact Assessment Review* stating that on average charcoal grilling produces three times more greenhouse gases than propane grilling. In conducting his research, Johnson used emission data from the

Intergovernmental Panel on Climate Change, public data from fuel producers, and measurements taken during experimental grilling sessions. His conclusion: "The overwhelming factors are that as a fuel, LPG [liquefied petroleum gas, or propane] is dramatically more efficient than charcoal in its production and considerably more efficient in cooking."[3]

The study found that each charcoal cookout session has about twice the carbon footprint of a propane cookout. The research further took into account that the process of making charcoal briquettes or lumps releases greater emissions than burning it. Charcoal is made by heating wood, which in many cases is the product of unsustainable logging, or by heating other biomass (organic matter that can be used as fuel) in an oxygen-free kiln, which emits greenhouse gases. The study took into consideration such secondary factors as the manufacture and transport of propane grills and tanks, the use of cylinders in propane grills, and the lighter fluids that many people use to ignite a charcoal fire for cooking.

The results of the study were widely reported in the media along with the recommendation that outdoor grilling enthusiasts switch to propane grilling to reduce emissions. Many reports also suggested that consumers who continue to charcoal grill should at least switch to eco-friendly charcoal carrying the Forest Stewardship Council or Rainforest Alliance certification logos. These charcoals, including the Cowboy Charcoal brand sold by Whole Foods and Lowe's, have the advantages of not using wood from trees in endangered woodlands, emitting fewer greenhouse gases, and not including additives that are released into the air and left on food during grilling.

Another environmentally friendly option may be a natural gas grill, which is connected to a fixed gas line. According to Virginia Natural Gas, natural gas grills produce 30 percent fewer greenhouse gas emissions than propane grills (the 2009 British study compared only propane to charcoal grills, and did not look at the overall environmental impact of natural gas grills). About

15 percent of gas grills in the United States are natural gas; the rest are propane.

Cleaning House

For decades, most people living in industrialized countries have relied on the latest products from the grocery or big box store to clean house. The result is an abundance of chemicals, stored in cans, bottles, and canisters, in laundry room, kitchen, and bathroom cabinets. Not only is the production of these chemicals bad for the environment, often leaching chemicals into the ground and air, but the transportation of the great variety of them to warehouses and stores requires the burning of fossil fuels—a larger carbon footprint than is necessary. They are bad for the environment inside our homes as well. According to an EPA study, indoor levels of pollutants (such as formaldehyde, chloroform, and styrene) can range from two to fifty times higher than outdoor levels—much of it from conventional cleaning supplies.

Many companies are making more home-cleaning products that are environmentally friendly, biodegradable, and nontoxic. Labels should be read carefully to make sure the product is actually earth friendly, however. Numerous manufacturers engage in "greenwashing," the act of misleading consumers about a company's green practices or the environmental benefits of its products. TerraChoice, an environmental marketing firm, conducted a 2009 study of products claiming to be eco-friendly and found that 98 percent of them engaged in some form of greenwashing. Even commercial cleaning products that are truly earth friendly have some environmental impact, however, requiring packaging and transportation to reach store shelves.

Some experts say that only the basics—water, white vinegar, baking soda, olive oil, club soda, and lemon juice, most of which can be found in the typical pantry—are needed to keep a home sparkling. Homemade solutions have several advantages: They require less packaging, and therefore less waste; they cost less; they are nontoxic—safe for humans, household pets, and the earth; and they often smell better than store-bought cleaning solutions. Furthermore, they are phosphate-free. Phosphates, which get into the water system by being washed down drains following dishwashing or clothes washing, nourish algae in waterways, thus depleting oxygen and upsetting ecosystems. As with their commercial counterparts, all natural household cleaners should be stored where children and pets cannot reach them, kept in airtight containers, and clearly labeled.

Reducing Water Consumption

Although consumption of water does not directly use energy or contribute to greenhouse gases, the delivery of water to homes does require energy. Furthermore, anytime water needs to be heated prior to use, energy is consumed, and that warm-water consumption carries a carbon footprint. The following tips will reduce household water consumption and the energy related to that consumption.

- Turning the dial on the water heater to 120°F (49°C) will allow for water warm enough for showering and washing, while reducing energy consumption.

- Wrapping a water heater with a blanket of insulation will reduce a heaters running time; checking with a heating expert or hardware store is advised.

- Showering uses substantially less water than bathing.

- Turning off water flow while soaping up or brushing teeth requires only a change in habit and will add up to savings over time.

- Low-flow showerheads and toilets save thousands of gallons of water per year; check the individual brand for specifics on savings and look for the WaterSense label when shopping for fixtures.

- Fixing leaks promptly will save water and money. To assess a household for leaks, turn off all water-using appliances and make sure all faucets are completely closed. Read the water meter, record it, and leave the house for several hours. If the water meter has changed during that absence, check all toilets, faucets, and plumbing for leaks.

• When it is time to replace a water heater, consider a tankless, on-demand heater, which is more efficient than its conventional counterpart. A tankless device heats water only when it is needed, whereas a conventional water heater keeps a supply of warm water on hand at all times, requiring greater energy use than on-demand systems.

Paper Products

Most in-home paper products are used for cleanup and personal hygiene. Reducing or eliminating the need for paper towels and paper napkins is simple and straightforward: switching to their cloth counterparts saves money and reduces environmental impact. Although it requires water and energy to wash cloth towels and napkins, using cloth reduces the demand for paper products, which saves trees, decreases manufacturing loads, and cuts down on the transportation required to move a steady stream of new paper products across the miles. When it comes to the bathroom, the best choice is to buy recycled paper products that have been whitened using an environmentally safe process that does not use chlorine bleach. Chlorine, when used in manufacturing processes, is an environmental threat because of the thousand or so compounds that result when chlorine reacts with substances that contain carbon. These chlorine-carbon compounds, or organochlorines, are toxic to the environment, are carcinogenic (cancer causing) to humans and animals, and deplete the earth's ozone layer.

According to Seventh Generation, manufacturer of recycled paper and other environmentally friendly products, the impact of choosing 100-percent-recycled paper products is great. According to the company's You Are Making a Difference campaign, if every U.S. household replaced just one box of eighty-five-sheet virgin fiber facial tissue with 100-percent-recycled tissues, it would save: 283,000 trees; 730,000 cubic feet (21,000 cubic meters) of landfill space or about 1,000 garbage trucks full; 102 million gallons (386 million liters) of water, a year's supply for 800 families of four. In addition, 17,000 pounds (8,000 kilograms) of chlorinated pollution would be avoided.

The figures are more impressive when it comes to switching out one roll of 500-sheet virgin fiber bathroom tissue with 100-percent-recycled toilet paper. If every U.S. household replaced just one roll, the nation would save: 423,900 trees; 1 million cubic feet (28,000 cubic meters) of landfill space or 1,600 garbage trucks full; and 153 million gallons (579 million liters) of water, a year's supply for 1,200 families of four. Seventh Generation cites similar figures for 100-percent-recycled paper towels—trees are saved, not as much landfill space is needed, and water can go where it is really needed.

Switching to recycled paper products does not need to be a wholesale change in the household: Even a partial adoption of recycled paper products will benefit the earth and contribute toward the effort to reduce global warming by sparing trees and water.

Many households with young children struggle with the issue of choosing diapers that have a low environmental impact. As with household napkins and towels, the more environmentally friendly choice is cloth, especially if it is organic. Cloth napkins, kitchen towels, and rags can all be laundered and used again; the same is true of the cloth diaper. But making the switch from the convenience of disposables is probably the most difficult transition a family can make in an effort to go green. Nevertheless, using cloth does save trees, water, and landfill space. If it is not possible or desirable to make the switch to a cloth diaper, environmentalists advise parents to choose disposables that do not contain chlorine. Biodegradable diapers provide another alternative; depending on materials, these diapers may be flushed, composted, or landfilled.

Recycled Paper

Using recycled paper at home, including reams for the printer as well as greeting cards and stationery, offers numerous benefits to the environment. Advantages include a reduction in methane emissions (a byproduct of standard paper production), extending the earth's fiber supply by sparing trees, saving landfill space; a reduction in CO_2 as a result of not using incinerators to burn paper waste, and an increase in carbon sequestration. Carbon sequestration describes the process of absorbing carbon faster than it is released. Because trees absorb carbon in the atmosphere, the more trees that are left standing, the higher the carbon sequestration rate. To put specifics behind this concept, the EPA provides the following data: For every ton of paper that is recycled, enough energy would be saved to power the average U.S. home for six months, 7,000 gallons (26,498 liters) of water would be saved, 3.3 cubic yards (2.5 cubic meters) of landfill space would be spared, and greenhouse gas emissions would be reduced by one metric ton of carbon equivalent. According to the nonprofit group Live Neutral, every pound of recycled paper prevents four pounds of carbon dioxide emissions. Looking for the products containing the highest available post-consumer content is advised.

The EPA has put forth a Resource Conservation Challenge with the goal to increase the United States' overall recycling rate to 40 percent by 2011; this figure includes all solid waste, not just paper. The U.S. forest, paper, and wood products industry, represented nationally by the American Forest & Paper Association (AF&PA), joined the EPA's commitment to recycling. The EPA reported in late 2008 that more paper was recovered in the United States for recycling (measured in terms of weight) than all other materials combined except for steel. The AF&PA set and tracked industry goals for voluntarily recovering paper. In 1990, the goal was set to recover 40 percent of the paper consumed in the United States; this goal was achieved in 1996. A goal of 50 percent recovery was then established, and it was met in 2003. At that time a new 55 percent goal was put forth, and it was ex-

Dedicated recycling bins help people keep bottles, plastic containers, paper, and other recyclables separate from trash. Andy Nelson/The Christian Science Monitor/Getty Images.

ceeded by 1 percent in 2007, five years ahead of schedule. The industry has been working toward a new goal of 60 percent recovery, which it hopes to meet by 2012. The result of these efforts is that significantly more paper is being recovered in the United States than is being landfilled. This represents a huge shift in the industry as well as in consumer habits—to recycle and choose recycled paper.

According to AF&PA, the brisk rise in paper recovery is attributable to strong demand overseas for U.S. recovered paper and solid gains in domestic consumption. As of late 2008, the AF&PA reported that more than three quarters of America's paper mills were using recovered fiber to make some or all of their products. Approximately 140 mills were using recovered paper exclusively. As a result, virtually all types of paper products contain some recycled fiber.

Finally, paper demand can be curtailed in the home. Because most American households have computers, paper use can be minimized through e-cards (greeting cards sent via the Internet) and e-mail, which help lessen the environmental impact of communicating with friends, family, and businesses.

Reducing Waste

There are several ways to reduce waste at home—to lessen how much rubbish and recycling are taken to the curb or incinerator or landfill each week. First is to reduce the amount of packaging that comes into the home. Whenever possible, buy in bulk (a practice discussed in more detail in Chapter 5: Food Choices). The fewer containers that are brought into the home, the fewer that will need to go out later.

The second way to reduce rubbish is to creatively reuse items whenever possible—to prolong the life of a container. Bags and boxes can be used again, as can some food containers as long as they are thoroughly washed and sanitized. The creative reuse of packaging is discussed in more detail in Chapter 7: Activism.

Keeping recycling receptacles handy in the home encourages everyone to toss empty cans, jars, papers, and other eligible containers into that bin instead of the trash bin, reducing what is headed to the landfill. Check municipal recycling rules to make sure nothing gets into the recycling bin that should not. According to the EPA, every ton of mixed paper recycled saves the energy equivalent of 185 gallons (700 liters) of gasoline. Recycling one ton of aluminum cans saves the energy equivalent of 1,665 gallons (6,303 liters) of gasoline.

Many unusual items can also be recycled, although not curbside. Electronics, batteries, ink cartridges, and cell phones can, and should, be recycled. Hazardous wastes, including toxic household cleaners, paints, and expired or unused medicine, should never be put in the trash. Most municipalities offer hazardous waste collection; checking with the local authority is advised.

Curbing Junk Mail Stopping junk mail will lessen the amount of paper that goes into the recycling bin each week and how much paper is needed to produce the mailings. It also saves the fossil fuel required to get the mailings into residential mailboxes. According to the U.S. Federal Trade Commission the flow into the home of unsolicited mail, including pre-approved credit card applications, can be stopped. Credit bureaus enable consumers to opt out of having pre-approved credit offers sent for five years; more information can be obtained at www.optoutprescreen.com.

U.S. consumers can also notify the three major credit bureaus that they do not want personal information about them shared for promotional purposes; this is an important step in eliminating unsolicited mail. Consumers can write a letter to each of the three major credit bureaus, specifically Experian, TransUnion, and Equifax.

To opt out of receiving unsolicited commercial mail from many national companies for five years, consumers can contact the Direct Marketing Association's Mail Preference Service. For a registration fee of $1, consumers can log their names onto a delete file that is made available to direct-mail marketers. This registration will not stop mailings from organizations that do not use the Mail Preference Service.

Composting Anyone with a yard or container garden can compost to reduce waste that would otherwise be headed to the landfill or down the garbage disposal. Composting, the decay of organic matter, is a natural process, and kitchen waste composting requires only a little effort. Furthermore, composting serves as a kind of carbon sink by storing, or sequestering, carbon in the soil instead of in the atmosphere.

An outdoor composting bin can be constructed or purchased, with models ranging from about $50 to $200 depending on materials and features. A covered compost pail or small bucket can be used in the kitchen to collect food waste. Kitchen composters are typically one gallon in size, and the best ones are fitted with a double carbon filter in the lid to help keep odors contained. No meat, fish, animal byproducts (such as butter and cheese), or oily foods should be added to the compost heap, but almost everything else, including vegetable scraps, fruit rinds and peels, grains, cereals, coffee grounds and filters, tea bags, and crushed eggshells, can go in. Once this matter is broken down, the yield is a nourishing blend to mix into soil and encourage plant growth in the garden. According to the EPA, composting kept almost 22 million tons of waste from landfills in the United States in 2007, the most recent year for which statistics were available.

Online Bill Payment Most utilities, banks, and credit card companies allow consumers to pay bills securely online, and most American households (63 percent in 2008) are doing so. Online calculators quantify the environmental impact of switching to electronic statements, bills, and payments. According to eBill's calculator, an individual who receives and pays ten bills per month will save 4 pounds (1.8 kilograms) of paper; keep 37 gallons (140 liters) of wastewater from being discharged into lakes, streams, and rivers; and avoid 151 pounds (68 kilograms) of greenhouse gases each year by receiving and paying bills online. The same amount of greenhouse gas could be saved by not driving a car for 146 miles (235 kilometers), planting two trees (and allowing them to grow for ten years), and preserving 20 square feet (1.85 square meters) of forest from deforestation.

Notes

1. ComEd, "Participate in Our Innovative Hourly Pricing Program," July 17, 2010, https://www.comed.com.
2. U.S. Department of Energy, "Appliances," January 22, 2009. www1.eere.energy.gov.
3. Eric Johnson, "Charcoal Versus LPG Grilling: A Carbon-Footprint Comparison," *Environmental Impact Assessment Review*, vol. 29, no. 6, November 2009, pp. 370–78.

CHAPTER 4

Transportation and Travel

According to the U.S. Environmental Protection Agency (EPA), transportation accounted for approximately 29 percent of total U.S. greenhouse gas emissions in 2006. The agency went on to report that transportation is the fastest-growing source of greenhouse gases in the United States, accounting for 47 percent of the net increase in total U.S. emissions since 1990. It is important to note that these estimates of transportation greenhouse gases do not include emissions from related processes, such as the extraction and refining of fuel and the manufacture of vehicles, which are also significant sources of domestic and international greenhouse gas emissions. Furthermore, the EPA reports that gasoline made from fossil fuels is the largest synthetic source of carcinogens (cancer-causing agents) and the leading source of toxic emissions.

Transportation emissions are rising because transportation is on the rise. This increase is a byproduct of the growing global population as well as consumer behavior. Some scientists expect the world's population to reach 9 billion around the year 2050 before leveling out. But long before then, changes in transportation can and should be made to curb greenhouse gas emissions around the world. In addition to the daily commute, the individual contributes to transportation-related emissions through car choice, vehicle maintenance, driving habits, and travel for business or leisure.

Fuel-Efficient Automobiles

In fall 2009 the U.S. government's Cash for Clunkers program, officially called Car Allowance Rebate System, took nearly seven hundred thousand gas-guzzling vehicles off the roads in fewer than thirty days as consumers replaced their old cars with more fuel-efficient models. The economic downturn and high fuel prices combined to put many Americans in the mindset of fuel efficiency for the first time since the energy crisis of the 1970s.

As automakers work to develop more fuel-efficient technologies, the federal government aims to help consumers find the most energy-efficient cars on the market. The Web site fueleconomy .gov, run by the U.S. Department of Energy (DOE), is a consumer guide to fuel economy. The site helps drivers find and compare cars, allowing searches by class, make, and miles per gallon. It also lists cars that do not run on gasoline or are flexible-fuel vehicles, which can run on gas or another type of fuel. The data provided for each car model include vehicle specs (range, size class, engine size, cylinders, transmissions, passenger volume, luggage volume), fuel economy, EPA air pollution score, and carbon footprint. Air pollution score and carbon footprint measure different types of vehicle emissions. Air pollutants harm human health or cause smog; carbon footprint measures greenhouse gas emissions (primarily CO_2) that cause climate change. Several alternative energies currently power vehicles or are in development; each is discussed below.

Ethanol Ethanol, which is produced domestically from corn and other crops (the plant matter in wheat, switch grass, corn stalks, rice straw, and wood chips) is cleaner than gasoline, emitting less carbon monoxide, particulate matter, and other ozone-forming pollutants. Flexible-fuel vehicles (FFVs), or flex cars, are designed to run on gasoline or a gasoline blend of up to 85 percent ethanol (E85). Except for a few engine and fuel-system modifications, they are identical to gasoline-only models. According to the DOE, FFVs have been produced since the 1980s, and dozens of models are currently available. Because FFVs look just like gasoline-only models, an individual may have an FFV and not know it; such cars are identified by a sticker on the inside of the car's fuel filler door or in the owner's manual. FFVs experience no loss in performance when operating on E85.

Ethanol does have disadvantages. Mass production of the alternative fuel could cause a shortage of corn available for food and would destroy habitat as more arable land would be required to grow the required amounts of corn. Furthermore, ethanol contains one third less energy than gasoline, which means mileage is 30 to 40 percent lower. The technology to mass-produce ethanol (or cellulose ethanol) from plant matter other than corn has not yet been developed.

Electric Cars and Hybrids Electric vehicles (EVs) are propelled by an electric motor or motors powered by rechargeable battery packs. Electric vehicles are more energy efficient than cars with internal combustion engines, converting 75 percent of the chemical energy from the batteries to power the wheels; internal combustion engines convert only 20 percent of the energy stored in gasoline to power the wheels. The DOE calls EVs environmentally friendly because they emit no tailpipe pollutants, although the power plant producing the electricity may emit pollutants. Electricity from nuclear-, hydro-, solar-, or wind-powered plants emits no air pollutants, but nuclear power plants do produce waste that poses a consequent disposal problem. Electric motors provide quiet, smooth operation and, in some cases, stronger acceleration than internal combustion engines; they also require less maintenance.

There are drawbacks to this technology. Most EVs can go only about 100 to 200 miles (160 to 320 kilometers) before recharging, whereas gasoline vehicles can travel more than 300 miles before refueling; fully recharging the battery pack can take

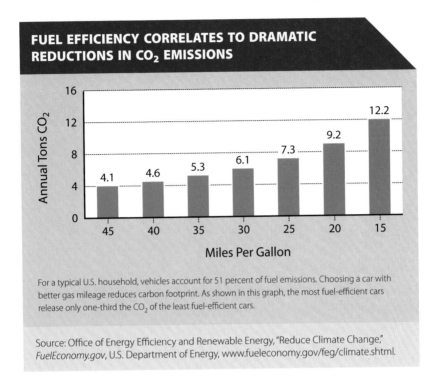

FUEL EFFICIENCY CORRELATES TO DRAMATIC REDUCTIONS IN CO_2 EMISSIONS

For a typical U.S. household, vehicles account for 51 percent of fuel emissions. Choosing a car with better gas mileage reduces carbon footprint. As shown in this graph, the most fuel-efficient cars release only one-third the CO_2 of the least fuel-efficient cars.

Source: Office of Energy Efficiency and Renewable Energy, "Reduce Climate Change," *FuelEconomy.gov*, U.S. Department of Energy, www.fueleconomy.gov/feg/climate.shtml.

four to eight hours (even a quick charge, to 80 percent capacity, can take thirty minutes); the battery packs are expensive and may need to be replaced one or more times during the life of the vehicle; and battery packs are heavy and large. Researchers are working on improved battery technologies to increase driving range and decrease recharging time, weight, and cost. These factors will determine the future of EVs.

Hybrid-electric vehicles (HEVs) combine the benefits of gasoline engines and electric motors. HEVs have a battery-powered electric motor that powers the car at slower speeds and a gas engine that kicks in at higher speeds. They can be configured to obtain different objectives, including improved fuel economy, increased power, and auxiliary power for electronic devices and power tools. Hybrids include the following advanced technologies:

- *Regenerative braking* The electric motor applies resistance to the drive train, causing the wheels to slow. The energy from the wheels turns the motor, which functions as a generator, converting energy normally wasted during coasting and braking into electricity, which is stored in a battery until needed by the electric motor.

- *Electric motor drive/assist* The electric motor provides additional power to assist the engine in accelerating, passing, or hill-climbing, thereby allowing a smaller, more efficient internal combustion engine to be used. In some vehicles, the electric motor alone provides power for low-speed (city) driving conditions, in which internal combustion engines are least efficient.

- *Automatic start/shutoff* This device automatically shuts off the engine when the vehicle comes to a stop and restarts it when the accelerator is pressed, preventing wasted energy during idling.

Biodiesel Biodiesel is a form of diesel fuel manufactured from vegetable oils, animal fats, or recycled restaurant greases. It is safe, biodegradable, and produces fewer air pollutants than petroleum-based diesel. Biodiesel can be used in its pure form (B100) or blended with petroleum diesel; common blends include B2 (2 percent biodiesel), B5 (5 percent), and B20 (20 percent). According to the DOE, B2 and B5 can be used safely in most diesel engines. Most vehicle manufacturers do not recommend using blends higher than B5 in diesel engines, and engine damage caused by higher blends is not covered by some manufacturer warranties.

Natural Gas Natural gas, a fossil fuel composed mostly of methane, is one of the cleanest-burning alternative fuels. It can be used in the form of compressed natural gas or liquefied natural gas to fuel cars and trucks. Dedicated natural gas vehicles are designed to run on natural gas only, whereas dual-fuel or bi-fuel vehicles can also run on gasoline or diesel. Dual-fuel vehicles allow users to take advantage of the widespread availability of gasoline or diesel but use a cleaner, more economical alternative when natural gas is available. Because natural gas is stored in high-pressure fuel tanks within the vehicle, dual-fuel vehicles require two separate fueling systems, which take up passenger and cargo space. Natural gas vehicles emit 60 to 90 percent less pollutants and 30 to 40 percent less greenhouse gas emissions than gasoline-powered engines. As of 2010, however, natural gas vehicles were not being produced commercially in large numbers (only one vehicle model was available in the United States); natural gas is less readily available than gasoline and diesel fuels, and it gets fewer miles on a tank of fuel.

Propane Propane or liquefied petroleum gas (LPG) is a clean-burning fossil fuel that can be used to power internal combustion engines. According to the DOE, LPG-fueled vehicles produce fewer toxic and air pollutants than vehicles powered by gasoline. LPG is usually less expensive than gasoline, and most LPG used in the United States comes from domestic sources. No LPG-fueled light-duty passenger cars or trucks were produced commercially in the United States after the 2004 model year, however. Like natural gas, LPG is not readily available and gets fewer miles per tank of fuel, both of which are challenges to the technology's long-term viability. Gasoline and diesel vehicles can be retrofitted to run on LPG in addition to conventional fuel. The LPG is stored in high-pressure fuel tanks, so separate fuel systems are needed in vehicles powered by both LPG and a conventional fuel such as gasoline.

Hydrogen/Fuel-Cell Vehicles: The Future of On-Road Transportation? Fuel-cell vehicles (FCVs) may someday revolutionize on-road transportation, according to the DOE. This emerging technology has the potential to significantly reduce energy use and harmful emissions, as well as U.S. dependence on foreign oil. Like hybrid-electric vehicles, FCVs are propelled by electric motors. But while hybrid-electric vehicles use electricity from an external source (and store it in a battery), FCVs create their own electricity. Onboard fuel cells create electricity through a chemical process using hydrogen fuel and oxygen from the air.

FCVs can be fueled with pure hydrogen gas stored onboard in high-pressure tanks. The vehicles also can be fueled with hydrogen-rich fuels such as methanol, natural gas, or even gasoline. But these fuels must first be converted into hydrogen gas by an onboard device called a reformer. FCVs fueled with pure hydrogen emit no pollutants, only water and heat. Ones using hydrogen-rich fuels and a reformer produce only small amounts of air pollutants. In addition, FCVs can be twice as efficient as similarly sized conventional vehicles and may also incorporate other advanced technologies to increase efficiency.

Daily Commuting

In the United States, as in other developed nations, commuting accounts for a good share of total transportation. A 2006 study published by the Transportation Research Board (TRB) of the National Academies reported that though work travel constituted only about 16 percent of total travel, there was dramatic growth in travel overall. Commuting was not diminishing—it was increasing both in the number of people getting to and from work and in duration. There are several ways the individual can reduce commuting-related greenhouse gas emissions.

A 10 percent increase in nationwide public transit ridership would save 135 million gallons of gas a year and create fewer greenhouse gases.

According to the TRB study, of the 128 million commuters in 2000, almost 100 million were in metropolitan areas, where public transportation options include buses, subways, and commuter trains. Yet less than 5 percent of Americans were using public transportation to travel to work. About half of the nation's public transportation commuters were found in ten major cities—Baltimore, Boston, Chicago, Houston, Los Angeles, New York, Philadelphia, San Francisco, Seattle, and Washington, D.C. Several environmental groups propose that, at the very least, commuters designate a certain day of each week to leave their cars at home. A 10 percent increase in nationwide public transit ridership would save 135 million gallons (511 million liters) of gas a year and create fewer greenhouse gases, according to the nonprofit organization Live Neutral. In addition to public transportation, alternate modes of commuting might include biking and walking—good for the environment and the individual.

Carpooling According to the TRB, driving by oneself continues to increase. The 2006 study indicates that solo drivers made up more than 80 percent of the total in fourteen states (with Michigan highest at more than 84 percent) and between 70 and 80 percent in thirty-three states. U.S. Census Bureau figures on commuting, released in 2007, echoed the TRB's findings: Driving a car to work was the foremost means of commuting for nine out of ten American workers, with nearly 88 percent of workers using an automobile to get to work. Most people, 77 percent, drove alone.

These numbers mean that at peak travel times in most of the nation, about eight of every ten vehicles had only the driver in them. Carpooling or vanpooling could quickly reduce these numbers, and the ripple effect would be tremendous. Not only would emissions be reduced because of fewer cars on the road, but traffic congestion would probably ease as well, reducing stop-

Following page: Passengers board a street car in downtown Seattle, one of ten U.S. cities that together account for about half of all public transportation use. Mary Knox Merrill/The Christian Science Monitor/Getty Images.

Calculating the Cost of Commuting

A 2006 Transportation Research Board study revealed that Michigan has more commuters driving alone than any other state. As part of Michigan's efforts to encourage drivers to share the commute, the state created a Cost to Commute Calculator so individuals can see exactly how much money, energy, and emissions can be saved through carpooling. By entering the number of days per month traveled to work, length (in miles) of daily round-trip commute, cost paid per gallon of gas, miles per gallon of the commuter's vehicle, and cost of parking, the individual can see the effect of removing his or her vehicle from the roads. The calculator determines estimated impact to air quality by reducing the amount of vehicle miles driven annually in the state, reducing the amount of volatile organic compounds emitted annually, reducing the amount of nitrogen oxide (NO_x) emitted annually, and reducing the amount of carbon dioxide (CO_2) emitted annually.

and-go conditions, shortening commute times, and increasing fuel efficiency, thereby further reducing emissions. In addition, the load on the roads would be lighter; without as much wear and tear, road reconstruction projects could be fewer and farther apart, again decreasing emissions by reducing the amount of heavy equipment on the nation's roadways as well as by keeping traffic moving.

Obstacles to carpooling include conflicting schedules and unexpected changes in participants' schedules, as well as safety concerns. To address these matters, many state governments run ride-sharing programs to help connect commuters, offering information at the department of transportation's Web site.

Alternative Work Schedules Flex time, compressed work weeks, and staggered shifts can all contribute to the reduction of peak period travel, thereby relieving traffic congestion, reducing travel times, and increasing the fuel efficiency of the vehicles on the road during peak travel. Alternative work schedules, particularly flex time, can have a positive environmental impact through the reduction of highway emissions. In flex-time programs, employers give their workers windows of time to arrive at and leave work, which some studies indicate may also facilitate ride sharing among employees. A compressed work week allows an employee to work forty hours over four days (4/40 schedule) or eighty hours over nine days (9/80 schedule), thereby reducing commuting by either one day per week or one day every other week. However, some studies have shown that compressed work weeks may reduce ride sharing and may encourage urban sprawl, lengthening commutes. Staggered shifts require employees to arrive and depart work in a similar manner to flex time, but without allowing employees to determine their own schedules. This alternative schedule may have the undesired effect of reducing ride sharing.

Telecommuting and Videoconferencing

Many employers are taking a closer look at telecommuting for workers who can do their jobs from a distance without impinging on the quality of their contribution. Even working at home one day a week or month will add up to a savings in commuting costs and emissions. Estimates indicate that telecommuting is a growing trend: The information technology research and advisory company Gartner Dataquest reported in 2008 that 25 percent of workers in the United States telecommuted in 2007; that number was estimated to have hit 27.5 percent in 2009.

According to the U.S. Travel Association, business travel constitutes 18 percent of total U.S. domestic person trips (a person trip is a trip made by a person by any mode or combination of modes of transportation, for any purpose); one in three of those trips involves air travel. There may be valid reasons an employee needs to travel for work, but emerging technology offers an alternative: Videoconferencing allows real-time interaction that is superior to telephone or instant messaging communications because of the ability to see the other people in the conference. Expressions and subtle nuances can be lost in teleconferencing or writing, but a live video feed provides the visual cues that are an important component of business communication. Some Web-based services, such as GoToMeeting and WebEx, also allow participants to share documents, collaborate, and demonstrate products and software during a meeting.

Around-Town Transportation

There are several ways to reduce vehicle emissions every day.

- *Getting regular checkups:* Experts advise that all cars, regardless of year and make, have regular maintenance performed. Changing the oil and air filter (estimated to save 800 pounds of carbon dioxide and $130 per year) and keeping tires properly inflated (estimated to save up to 250 pounds of carbon dioxide and $840 per year) are simple procedures that help a vehicle run at its most efficient and maximize mileage.

- *Taking it easy:* Driving at 75 miles per hour (121 kilometers per hour) uses 13 percent more gas than does going 65 miles per hour (105 kilometers per hour). Aggressive driving requires more braking and keeps the car in a lower, less efficient gear.

- *Turning off the AC:* Running the air conditioning increases fuel consumption by 13 to 21 percent, according to Live Neutral. Rolling down car windows, however, can also make a car less fuel efficient, depending on speed of travel. In some weather conditions, the vehicle vents will keep the car interior comfortable for passengers and save fuel.

- *Reducing the baggage:* Each 100 pounds (45 kilograms) in a car increases gas consumption 1 to 2 percent.

- *Minimizing idling:* Idling a car wastes money and energy, and it increases emissions. Experts recommend no more than 30 seconds of idling, unless the car is in traffic.

- *Coordinating transportation:* Consolidating trips reduces miles traveled overall. This means planning errands ahead of time and communicating with other members of the household to coordinate transportation needs.
- *Avoiding peak travel times:* If errands can be run at off-times, they will take less time and require less fuel. Traveling when it is not commuter rush hour is advised whenever possible.
- *Carpooling:* Sharing a ride with a neighbor reduces the number of cars on the road. Neighborhood car pools to and from schools and athletic events are good examples of coordinating transportation to reduce emissions.
- *Taking a day off from driving:* Designating a no-car day every week reduces the number of cars on the road, prompts the household to consolidate travel the rest of the week, and encourages alternate forms of transportation, including walking and biking.

Vacationing

Leisure travel accounts for most trips, and in such circumstances the individual makes all the choices. Driving to one's destination—or taking the train or bus—is more energy efficient than flying. If flying is a must, nonstop flights are more carbon friendly than ones with stopovers as most fuel is expended during takeoff and landing. Once at the destination, travelers can reduce emissions by choosing public transportation options, if available, or by sharing rides with fellow travelers.

The options for green travel are growing, with eco-friendly lodging emerging as a new hospitality industry. Green lodging aims to be as carbon neutral as possible—in building design, selection of furnishings and linens, food and beverage offerings, and amenities. Regardless of the type of hotel that is chosen, guests can reduce their carbon footprint by reusing towels and bed linens and by turning off lights and the heat or air condition-ing when leaving the room.

Because green travel is something of an oxymoron (the most carbon-neutral option would be to stay at home), the concept is more appropriately called sustainable travel. The U.S. Travel Association's Travel Green Web site, at www.travelgreen.org, is a starting point for learning more about sustainable vacation plan-ning and ideas.

CHAPTER 5

Food Choices

Health and environmental impacts have contributed to important shifts in consumer food choices, with more buyers considering where their food originates, how it is grown, and how it gets to the plate. By the time food reaches the individual, it has been on a journey and has a carbon footprint of its own. That footprint ranges from almost nothing—the tomato that was harvested in the backyard organic garden—to substantial—the frozen dinner in its individual serving tray. The term food miles (or food kilometers) refers to the distance a food travels from where it was grown or raised to where it is purchased by the consumer.

Increasingly, consumers are seeking out organic and whole foods (that is, natural, unprocessed, and unrefined), and they are paying more for them at the cash register, not only because they believe organic and whole foods to be better for their bodies but because they believe them to be better for the environment. The process seems very simple. But food production and distribution are complex matters, particularly when considered as part of reducing individual environmental impact.

Emissions of greenhouse gases related to food production, distribution, and consumption occur primarily whenever there is energy use. According to researchers Martin C. Heller and Gregory A. Keoleian of the University of Michigan's School of Natural Resources and Environment, the breakdown of energy use in the food system is as follows (all percentages are rounded to the nearest whole number):

- On-farm production: 20 percent of the total (with 40 percent of this amount going toward the production of chemical fertilizers and pesticides, or "indirect inputs")
- Transportation: 14 percent
- Processing: 16 percent
- Packaging: 7 percent
- Retail: 4 percent
- Commercial food service: 7 percent
- Household storage (refrigeration) and preparation (cooking, baking, toasting, heating): 32 percent

In considering the role of the individual in climate change, it is important to look at the relevant aspects of food production—farm production, transportation, processing, packaging, and food preparation. Although transportation, at 14 percent, does not account for the highest energy consumption in the food system, it is a good starting point.

Eating Locally: The Locavore Movement

The basic principle followed by a locavore is to eat foods harvested locally, usually within a 100-mile (160-kilometer) radius. These foods might be grown in a home garden, raised on an area farm, or purchased in season from a farmers market. According to locavore ideals, if a food item cannot be procured locally, then the next best choices are to buy from a local food business or from a regional, preferably family-operated, farm—one that may be outside the 100-mile radius but is not far away. According to the Worldwatch Institute, an independent research organization in Washington, D.C., the local-food movement has been gaining momentum in developed countries since it emerged around 2000. In the United States, sales of locally grown foods amounted to about $4 billion in 2002 and could reach as much as $7 billion by 2011.

Oily Food? In her book *Animal, Vegetable, Miracle*, Barbara Kingsolver chronicles her family's first year of eating strictly

DISTANCES TRAVELED BY FRESH PRODUCE

			Number of States Supplying This Item	Percent of Total from Mexico
	Each truck represents about 500 miles of distance traveled.			
Grapes		2,143 miles	1	7
Broccoli		2,095 miles	3	3
Asparagus		1,671 miles	5	37
Apples		1,555 miles	8	0
Sweet Corn		813 miles	16	7
Squash		781 miles	12	43
Pumpkins		233 miles	5	0

This chart shows the average distance several produce items were transported by truck to Chicago Terminal Market. Locally grown foods have a smaller carbon footprint than foods transported over distances, unless there is an energy-intensive input somewhere else in the food's life cycle (such as hothouse-grown tomatoes).

Source: "How Far Do Your Fruit and Vegetables Travel?," *Leopold Letter*, Leopold Center for Sustainable Agriculture, Iowa State University, April 2002. www.leopold.iastate.edu.

local—so local that most of the family's foodstuffs came from its own garden, hen house, or turkey coop. As contributor Steven L. Hopp (Kingsolver's husband) explains, the family made the change after concluding their food was "oily": "Americans put almost as much fossil fuel into our refrigerators as our cars. We're consuming about 400 gallons of oil [equivalent] a year per citizen—about 17% of our nation's energy use—for agriculture, a close second to our vehicular use."[1]

This 400-gallons-of-oil figure Hopp and other locavores quote originated in the 1994 paper "Food, Land, Population and the U.S. Economy" by leading scientists David Pimentel and Mario Giampietro. The two professors, Pimentel from Cornell University and Giampietro from Rome's Istituto Nazionale della Nutrizione, made a comprehensive assessment of U.S. population growth and its impact on American agricultural productivity. Their study was commissioned by the Carrying Capacity Network, a Washington, D.C.–based nonprofit that focuses on the interrelated nature of the economy, population growth, and environmental degradation.[2]

How is all this oil consumed? First, farmers use energy to produce crops. This energy is classified as either direct or indirect. Direct energy powers tractors and other farm machinery with fossil fuels. Indirect energy accounts for fertilizers, pesticides, feeds, and grains—also called agricultural inputs. These inputs must be manufactured, packaged, stored, and transported—all requiring energy consumption and therefore resulting in greenhouse gases.

Second, commercial farming today relies on economies of scale—industrial growers concentrated by region. According to the U.S. Department of Agriculture's (USDA's) 2003 data, 8 percent of all farms accounted for about 68 percent of agricultural production. In the United States, most wheat comes from the plains states, corn and soybeans from the Midwest, and fresh vegetables from California. This national system relies on large quantities of fossil fuels to transport food to the consumer.

Third, processed foods add to fossil fuel consumption by requiring shipment of a variety of ingredients to factories. According to Heller and Keoleian's research, processing and packaging foods accounts for 23 percent of the energy used in the U.S. food production system. In 2005, Iowa State University researchers at the Leopold Center for Sustainable Agriculture found that the milk, sugar, and strawberries used to make a carton of strawberry yogurt collectively traveled 2,211 miles (3,558 kilometers) just to arrive at the processing plant. Once at the food processing site, more energy is consumed to prepare, cook, package, and refrigerate or freeze the finished product before it is shipped to warehouses and stores.

Fourth, the global food market requires burning fossil fuels. Atlantic salmon, Hawaiian pineapples, and Italian wines are year-round staples in most grocery stores, and all have usually traveled great distances to get there. According to the USDA, more than $195 billion of agricultural products crossed U.S. borders as exports ($115 billion) or imports ($80 billion) in 2008. An astonishing calculation of food miles emerged in 1992 after a Swedish study totaled the distance that the ingredients of a typical Swedish breakfast (apple, bread, butter, cheese, coffee, cream, orange juice, and sugar) had traveled: The distance estimated for the meal was equivalent to the circumference of the Earth. There are environmental costs to moving food across the miles—in the fossil fuel burned by trains, trucks, and ships in moving food; in the associated greenhouse gas emissions; and in the refrigeration that is required to keep food fresh as it travels.

Food Miles Considered Brian Halweil, senior researcher at the Worldwatch Institute, covers modern food matters in his book *Eat Here: Homegrown Pleasures in a Global Supermarket.* According to Halweil, food in the United States now travels 25 percent farther to reach the dinner table—and in the United Kingdom 50 percent farther—than it did just two decades ago. Halweil argues that globetrotting food is bad for the health of economies and people alike, while eating local and encouraging regional self-sufficiency is good for the environment and for humans.

Produce trucked from 100 miles away or shipped by rail from 1,000 miles away would have about the same carbon footprint.

Iowa State University's Leopold Center researchers have extensively analyzed food miles, looking at the transport of food through local, regional, and conventional food distribution systems. In 2001 they reported that food transported through a conventional distribution system—which is to say a national network using semitrailer trucks to haul food to large grocery stores—traveled an average of 1,546 miles (about 2,488 kilometers). But locally distributed food traveled an average of only 44.6 miles (72 kilometers) to market. When considering only produce, the local food traveled an average distance of 37.9 miles (61 kilometers), whereas the produce would probably travel an average of 1,638 miles (2,636 kilometers) if it were distributed through conventional sources. The Iowa team concluded that the conventional food distribution system used four to seventeen times more fuel and emitted five to seventeen times more CO_2 than the local and regional (statewide) systems.

The Leopold researchers further concluded that the "infrastructure and decision-making in the current food system are based on profitability, and often do not take into account external environmental or community costs." They went on to state that "food produced within local or regional food systems travels fewer miles (from farm to point of sale) than the food produced within a conventional system. The shorter transportation distances for these local and state-based regional food systems led to reduced transportation fuel use and CO_2 emissions compared to the conventional system."[3]

Is Local Best? Food miles are one factor in determining food's environmental impact. According to Rich Pirog of Iowa State's Leopold Center, "Food miles are a good measure of how far food has traveled. But they're not a very good measure of the food's environmental impact."[4] The mode of transportation is also a factor: Trains move freight ten times more efficiently, ton for ton, than do trucks. According to this conversion, produce trucked from 100 miles away or shipped by rail from 1,000 miles away would have about the same carbon footprint.

The way food is grown also affects its environmental impact. Swedish researcher Annika Carlsson-Kanyama has conducted numerous studies into food and its greenhouse gas emissions, some with surprising results. In one—reported in *World Watch* magazine in 2008[5]—she found that it was preferable for her countrymen to buy Spanish tomatoes rather than their home-grown counterparts because the Spanish tomatoes were grown in open fields while the Swedish varieties were cultivated in greenhouses that had to be warmed using fossil fuel. Yet even in this one example there are possible variables. First, Scandinavian greenhouses could be warmed using renewable energy sources, thereby reducing the carbon footprint of locally or regionally grown tomatoes. Second, as the climate changes, it is possible that Spain's growing conditions could become too hot and dry to produce the tomatoes it is known for, requiring irrigation systems—and energy—to continue the crop.

The comprehensive analysis of the greenhouse gas emissions of food requires that not just transportation is considered, but food production and all the variables of its production—its entire life cycle. Food miles are but one part of that analysis. As Pirog notes, "It is true that if you're comparing exact systems, the same food grown in the same way, then obviously, yes, the food transported less will have a smaller carbon footprint."[6]

The locavore movement has caused many people to think about where their food originates. When it comes to producing and distributing food in a sustainable and globally responsible manner, eating local is part of the solution. Farmers markets, roadside stands, and community-supported agriculture programs (CSAs) are all ways to support a local food system. This practice also means eating foods when they are in season— tomatoes, basil, leafy greens, and berries in summer; apples, hard squashes, and potatoes and other root vegetables in winter.

Organic Foods

The USDA defines organic food as "produced by farmers who emphasize the use of renewable resources and the conservation of soil and water to enhance environmental quality for future generations. Organic meat, poultry, eggs, and dairy products come from animals that are given no antibiotics or growth hormones. Organic food is produced without using most conventional pesticides; fertilizers made with synthetic ingredients or sewage sludge; bioengineering; or ionizing radiation."[7] Furthermore, in order to bear the USDA-certified organic label, a government-approved certifier must inspect the farm where the food is grown to make sure the farmer is following all the rules necessary to meet USDA organic standards. A product needs to be certified as at least 95 percent organic before it can carry the USDA's seal. And when it comes to processed or prepared foods, the companies that handle or process organic food before it gets to the supermarket or restaurant must be certified by the USDA as well. Foods carry a variety of labels and terms:

- 100 Percent Organic: These products are completely organic or made of all organic ingredients.
- Organic: These products are at least 95 percent organic.
- Made with Organic Ingredients: Typically, these are products that contain at least 70 percent organic ingredients. The USDA Certified Organic seal cannot be used.
- All Natural, Free-Range, Hormone-Free: These terms refer to production methods but do not equate to organic. For example, eggs may be labeled as all natural and free-range,

but unless the hens are consuming a strictly organic diet and are raised according to organic standards, they cannot carry the organic label.

Opinions abound about organic foods, with some consumers perceiving them on the plus side as more nutritious, more healthful, safer, and more flavorful than their conventionally produced counterparts, and others thinking of them as expensive, only for the select few, and unsustainable. The legitimacy of these claims bears consideration. But the question at hand is this: Are organic foods better for the environment? The answer is yes, in terms of reducing inputs (fertilizers and other synthetic chemicals) and outputs (air pollution and runoff) as well as in carbon sequestration (a natural process by which carbon is removed from the air and trapped in the soil, where it is beneficial). According to David Pimentel of Cornell University, U.S. agriculture emits 925 billion pounds (420 billion kilograms) of carbon each year through crop and livestock production.[8] The Natural Resources Defense Council explains that "pesticide or fertilizer laden runoff from farmlands washes into rivers, lakes, and streams, contaminating waterways, and destroying habitat. Many pesticides are also toxic to health, and have been linked to respiratory problems, neurological disorders such as Parkinson's disease, cancer and reproductive problems."[9] The organization Live Neutral cites research that has shown that organic soils contain up to 28 percent more carbon than other soils. Research on this topic abounds. The Rodale Institute conducted a long-running comparison of organic and conventional cropping systems. Its report, published in 2003, concluded that organic farming methods are much more effective at removing carbon dioxide from the atmosphere and fixing it as beneficial organic matter in the soil, and with substantial results: "If only 10,000 medium-sized farms in the U.S. converted to organic production, they would store so much carbon in the soil that it would be equivalent to taking 1,174,400 cars off the road, or reducing car miles driven by 14.62 billion miles."[10]

Organic Foods: Myth and Reality

myth Organic foods are no healthier than non-organic foods.

reality Wrong: Food produced organically contains fewer contaminants. Some scientific studies have shown that there are more nutrients in organically produced food.

myth Organic farming increases the risk of food poisoning.

reality False: Organic farming can actually reduce the risk.

myth Organic farming uses pesticides that damage the environment.

reality Untrue: Organic farming systems rely upon prevention rather than cure, minimizing the need for pesticides.

myth Consumers are paying too much for organic food.

reality Not so: Crop rotations, organic animal feed and welfare standards, the use of good husbandry instead of agri-chemicals, and the preservation of natural habitats all result in organic food costing more to produce. Non-organic food appears to be cheaper but in fact consumers pay for it three times over—first over the counter, second via taxation (to fund agricultural subsidies) and third to remedy the environmental pollution caused by intensive farming practices.

myth Organic food cannot feed a hungry world.

reality False: Intensive farming destroys the fertility of the land and is unsustainable. Organic methods help labor-rich but cash-poor communities to produce food sustainably.

myth Organic farming is unkind to animals.

reality Far from it: Animal welfare and the freedom to behave naturally is central to organic livestock standards.

SOURCE: *Organic Food and Farming: Myth and Reality*, **Soil Association and Sustain: The Alliance for Better Food and Farming, 2001.**

Is it practical for all farms to become organic? Many agricultural experts say that the goal should not be to convert all farms to completely organic operations, but rather to move conventional agriculture to accept more organic practices, such as soil conservation techniques, thereby reducing the environmental impact of the globe's largest agricultural producers and moving toward a more sustainable agriculture model. A major emphasis should be placed on reducing and minimizing the use of energy-intensive inputs that go into conventional agricultural production. The matter returns to direct versus indirect energy in agriculture. The manufacture of fertilizers and pesticides is an energy-intensive business, and one that commercial farms have relied on steadily since their introduction. According to the USDA, from the mid-1960s through 1981, commercial fertilizer use doubled, peaking at just over 23 million metric tons (just over 25 million tons). Since the early 1980s, commercial fertilizer use has remained at about 22 million metric tons in the United States. The same is true globally: Fertilizer use peaked in the 1980s before leveling off around 140 million metric tons (157 million tons). Not only is energy used during the production of agricultural chemicals, resulting in greenhouse gas emissions, but greenhouse gases are byproducts of the industrial processes themselves. When fertilizers, for example, are manufactured, greenhouse gases are released into the atmosphere. The application of synthesized fertilizers and pesticides also results in the release of Greenhouse gases. According to the EPA, agricultural soil management activities such as fertilizer application and other cropping practices were the largest source of U.S. nitrogen oxide (NO_x) emissions in 2007, accounting for 67 percent. And NO_x, over a hundred-year period, has almost 300 times more impact per unit weight than carbon dioxide, according to the Intergovernmental Panel on Climate Change.

The individual who opts for organic is choosing the food product that has most likely used less energy, required fewer of the earth's resources, and emitted fewer greenhouse gases than its conventionally produced counterpart. Consumers who are able to purchase organics are voting with their wallets, demonstrating to grocery stores, food companies, and agricultural producers that there is demand for these products. And such demand would be hard to ignore: According to the Organic Trade Association, a membership-based business association for the organic industry in North America, U.S. sales of organic food and beverages grew from $1 billion in 1990 to an estimated $20 billion in 2007. Globally, the demand for organic products has also been on the rise. According to the Organic Monitor (a U.K.-based provider of data to organic operators), global sales of organic food and drink reached $46 billion in 2007. The rate was anticipated to slow in countries affected by the financial crisis that began around 2008.

Whole Foods

The term "whole foods" describes natural, unprocessed, and unrefined foods—foods that arrive in the kitchen looking much as they did when they left the farm. Consumer demand for whole foods declined after industrialization. Commercially produced canned foods were introduced in the late 1800s, quick-frozen foods were developed in the 1920s, and the so-called TV dinner was invented in the 1950s. All of these products made in-home dinner preparation easier and provided the home cook with a greater variety of ingredients and options. As a result, the diet of people living in industrialized nations steadily changed, with more processed foods becoming part of the daily diet.

Canned, frozen, and other packaged foods usually have larger carbon footprints than their whole-food counterparts. The ingredients that are used to manufacture a processed food all must be transported to a food plant, where energy is consumed to make the final product before it is put into a human-made container and shipped again, this time to warehouses and grocery stores. It might not be possible or even desirable to eliminate all processed foods from the diet, but limiting their consumption does yield the benefit of reducing emissions. Whole foods, which is to say unprocessed and unrefined foods, are also better for the human body as they are loaded with nutrients (vitamins, minerals, and phytochemicals) and contain no synthetic preservatives or chemicals.

Reducing Meat Consumption

Gas emitted from livestock as part of the digestive process is a major source of methane, one of the greenhouse gases. Roughly one third of the world's methane emissions is produced by bacteria that live in the digestive systems of cattle, sheep, and goats. Scientists are working to find solutions to the problem of livestock methane emissions. For example, a 2009 study, conducted by researchers at University College Dublin in Ireland, found that including 2 percent fish oil in the diet of cattle reduced the amount of methane the animals released. More research is under way.

Methane release is only one of the environmental impacts of a meat-based diet, however. According to the University of Michigan's Center for Sustainable Systems, a meat-based diet (defined as 28 percent of caloric intake from animal products) requires twice as much energy to produce as a vegetarian diet does. More than half the grain that is grown goes to feeding livestock. And grain production requires transportation (which consumes fossil fuels and emits greenhouse gases), farmland (which involves deforestation), and pesticide use.

For these reasons, environmental organizations concerned about global warming have been urging consumers to eat less meat. But many food, agriculture, and environmental experts view this encouraged vegetarianism as impractical and unsustainable. Livestock industry supporters say consumer preferences and tastes cannot be altered to eliminate beef, lamb, and other meats from their diets, and that doing so would devastate entire industries, upon which the livelihood of many producers depends.

The fact is that meat consumption is up in general. According to the USDA, in 2006 Americans ate 220 pounds (100 kilograms) of meat per person compared to 178 pounds (81 kilograms) per person in 1970. This increase correlates to an overall increase in U.S. caloric intake per person, a contributor to the obesity epidemic.

If consumers reduced meat intake, the environmental impact would be favorable in terms of land use, water use, and emissions. According to the Union of Concerned Scientists, eating less meat is one of the most effective environmental choices. The nonprofit Live Neutral puts specifics behind this conclusion: By giving up beef once a week for a year, one person would save more than 70 pounds (32 kilograms) each of grain and topsoil, as well as 40,000 gallons (151,416 liters) of water. The actual amount of water saved may be greater, depending on how much beef a person considers to be a serving size; it also depends on what the individual is consuming instead of beef. But there is no argument that livestock production is a water-intensive industry. According to research from Cornell University, growing the grain to feed cattle requires 12,000 gallons (45,425 liters) of water for every pound (half a kilogram) of beef.[11]

Reducing Food Waste and Excess Consumption

A simple way to help the environment is to require less of it. By reducing the amount of food that is thrown away, a consumer reduces household demand for food in the first place. Doing so, in turn, reduces fossil fuel use, deforestation, and water use. According to Live Neutral, the average family of four wastes $600 of food a year. Careful planning is the key component to minimizing food waste. Monitoring use-by dates and freshness, scrutinizing portion sizes, and planning to eat leftovers are all effective methods for decreasing the amount of food that is discarded.

Reducing caloric intake to the appropriate amount per day benefits the body and theearth. According to the USDA, the average American consumed 2,700 calories per day in 2000, an increase of 24.5 percent from 1970. This increase resulted in an obesity epidemic (with about two thirds of the U.S. population being overweight or obese, including a rising population of overweight and obese children) as well as in placing a disproportionate per-person demand on agricultural resources. Although many adults believe an appropriate daily caloric intake to be between 1,800 and 2,000, the range is actually much greater, from about 1,500 to 3,200 calories per day. Daily caloric intake should be geared toward an individual's gender, age, height, weight, and daily activity level. Caloric intake calculators can be found online, including at the Mayo Clinic Web site and WebMD. When it comes to appropriate caloric intake for children, pediatricians are the best advisers.

Packaging

Consumers bring a variety of food products in a variety of packages into their homes. The basic categories for food container materials are flexible plastics (film lids and wrappers, bags, pouches); rigid plastics (bottles, trays, pots, tubs); cardboard (cartons, multi-packs); glass (bottles, jars); and metal (cans, trays). Many of these packages can be reused or recycled. The best practice is to reuse a thoroughly cleaned container several times before recycling it.

But some packaging cannot be reused or recycled—once discarded, it heads straight to the landfill. Landfill garbage produces methane, a greenhouse gas twenty-one times more potent than carbon dioxide. Transporting and incinerating garbage releases carbon dioxide as well.

According to the Environmental Protection Agency (EPA), municipal solid waste in the United States has been on the rise since 1960. Municipal solid waste includes packaging, food scraps, grass clippings, old furniture, computers, tires, and appliances. It does not include industrial, hazardous, or construction waste. But the per capita figure has leveled off since 1990, holding steady around 4.5 to 4.6 pounds (20 to 21 kilograms) of waste per person per day (the overall rise is attributable to an increase in the population). In 2007 Americans recovered 63 million tons of waste (excluding composting) through recycling. This amount is 1.9 million more tons than the year before. These figures paint an unclear picture—Americans are improving their recycling habits but still discarding a great amount of waste.

Food packaging adds up quickly, simply because food is brought into the home regularly and in quantity. By reducing the number of containers that are brought into the home to begin with, less packaging will need to be disposed of later. The best practice is to buy items in bulk or in larger sizes, then put them into smaller, reusable containers at home. Applesauce, crackers, and chips are examples of items that can be bought in single-serving containers as well as in large, bulk sizes that can be served as needed. Perhaps buying in bulk is not always possible or convenient; single-serving sizes will sometimes make sense. But even if the individual buys in bulk most of the time, less waste will head to recycling centers or to the landfill.

Tap Water Instead of Bottled Water Individually bottled water swept the beverage marketplace during the 1990s and early 2000s, making it convenient to carry a bottle of water anywhere. Bottled water became so popular that it was the subject of an episode of the TV sitcom *Seinfeld*, whose characters argued about the superiority of one brand over another. An industry had emerged, peaking in 2007 when U.S. sales surpassed $11 billion. But in 2008, after years of double-digit increases, sales were flat. Industry analysts attributed the stagnation in bottled water sales to economic downturn, which had consumers opting for far cheaper tap water (costing just a fraction of a penny per glass). But environmentalists hoped the change was also in

Following page: Plastic bottles and other excess packaging have become a major environmental nuisance, floating at sea and clogging many of the world's waterways. Dimitar Dilkoff/AFP/ Getty Images.

response to consumers' heightened awareness of bottled water's environmental costs.

The environmental costs include the production of plastic bottles, distribution, and disposal—all of which require fossil fuel and the resulting emissions. The tremendous problem of bottled water disposal came to light in 1997 when American sailor Charles Moore made a startling discovery while returning from Hawaii to Los Angeles on his yacht: He found his craft in the midst of an enormous floating garbage patch, much of it consisting of empty plastic beverage bottles. Day after day, Moore sailed through the rubbish, thousands of miles from land. The floe is now known as "the great Pacific garbage patch" and the "trash vortex." It exists thousands of miles from land in the North Pacific gyre, an area where the ocean circulates slowly because of little wind and extreme high pressure systems, holding the garbage in place. The area has been estimated to be roughly twice the size of Texas. It is not solid trash, but rather a soup of litter—much of it plastic. The vast expanse of debris is essentially the world's largest rubbish dump. And researchers believe it is not the only such garbage floe.

A 2007 *New York Times* editorial summed up the environmental impact of the bottled water habit:

> Water bottles, like other containers, are made from natural gas and petroleum. The Earth Policy Institute in Washington, D.C. has estimated that it takes about 1.5 million barrels of oil to make the water bottles Americans use each year. That could fuel 100,000 cars a year instead. And, only about 23 percent of those bottles are recycled, in part because water bottles are often not included in local redemption plans that accept beer and soda cans. Add in the substantial amount of fuel used in transporting water, which is extremely heavy, and the impact on the environment is anything but refreshing.[12]

The beverage industry responded to concerns over plastic bottles by reducing the plastic content of the individual bottle.

This is a help, but it is not a solution. What can the individual do? Choose tap water. Many studies have shown it is of equal and sometimes better quality than bottled. Furthermore, the consumer avoids ingesting trace chemicals from the plastic and saves money—a substantial amount of money if a person is abiding by the recommendation to drink eight eight-ounce glasses of water every day. The same goes for teas and coffees, water-based beverages that can be made at home. Rather than purchasing individually packaged drinks, beverages can be brewed at home and poured into reusable bottles or thermoses.

Reusable Shopping Bags Carrying reusable shopping bags to the store eliminates the need for both plastic and paper bags. All disposable bags come at a cost to the environment. Paper bags are made of a renewable resource, can be recycled curbside, and will break down in a landfill, unlike plastic, but they deplete Earth's supply of trees. Plastic bags use less energy to produce, generate less solid waste (per bag), and generate fewer emissions than paper bags (because they do not weigh as much in transport), but they are petroleum-based and do not biodegrade.

In 1977, North Carolina inventor Gordon Dancy developed the compact, grocery-style plastic bag as a replacement for the then-standard paper grocery sack. Dancy did so in response to the logging of trees in tropical countries, economic inflation, and the public's heightened environmental consciousness after the celebration of the first Earth Day in 1969. But Dancy eventually perceived the problem with plastic bags littering the environment and clogging landfills, and he reportedly regretted having invented the bags. With stores around the globe handing their customers billions of plastic bags every day, trillions of bags are littering the environment, including waterways, and clogging landfills. In 2008, *National Geographic* reported, "From Australia to the U.K., and all across the U.S., politicians and corporations are pondering banning or taxing plastic bags."[13] Indeed, by 2010 governments around the world had chosen to ban or tax single-use plastic bags, or charge consumers for them.

Reusable shopping bags are widely available and inexpensive. Making a habit of keeping them handy and carrying them to the store whenever shopping will help reduce demand for disposable bags, curb their production, reduce emissions, and cut waste.

In-Home Food Preparation

About one third of energy used in the food system is burned in the home—through refrigeration and preparation. But there are ways to reduce energy consumption here as well, and without adopting a raw diet. First, if a stove, oven, microwave, or refrigerator is old, consider replacing it; today's models are more energy efficient than they were even a few years ago. Second, when shopping for new kitchen appliances, look for the Energy Star label to make sure that the model is efficient. Also, it is important to make sure the appliance suits the needs of the household; most home kitchens do not require restaurant-grade appliances, which are larger than home appliances (and require more resources to manufacture and ship), and often require more energy to operate. This need is especially true of commercial ranges, which require additional ventilation as well. Third, cook smart by planning meals around using as few appliances as possible as well as by maximizing microwave use; the microwave oven is the home kitchen's most energy-efficient means of cooking. Various means of saving energy in the kitchen are discussed more fully in Chapter 2: Daily Living at Home.

Notes

1. Barbara Kingsolver, with Steven L. Hopp and Camille Kingsolver, *Animal, Vegetable, Miracle*. New York: HarperCollins, 2007, p. 5.
2. David Pimentel and Mario Giampietro, *Food, Land, Population and the U.S. Economy*, Washington, D.C.: The Carrying Capacity Network, 1994.
3. Rich Pirog et al., "Food, Fuel, and Freeways: An Iowa Perspective on How Far Food Travels, Fuel Usage, and Greenhouse Gas Emissions," *Leopold Center for Sustainable Agriculture*, June 2001. www.leopold.iastate.edu.

4. Quoted in Sarah DeWeerdt, "Is Local Food Better?" *World Watch*, May/June 2008. www.worldwatch.org/node/6064.
5. DeWeerdt, "Is Local Food Better?"
6. Quoted in DeWeerdt, "Is Local Food Better?"
7. U.S. Department of Agriculture, "Organic Food Standards and Labels: The Facts," June 2007. www.nal.usda.gov.
8. Laura Sayre, "Organic Farming Combats Global Warming," *Rodale Institute*, October 10, 2003. www.rodaleinstitute.org.
9. National Resources Defense Council, "The Benefits of Organic Food," November 11, 2009. www.nrdc.org.
10. Sayre, "Organic Farming Combats Global Warming."
11. Cornell University, "End Irrigation Subsidies and Reward Conservation, Cornell Water-Resources Study Advises / Burgeoning World Population and Global Warming Threaten Business-As-Usual, but Change Is Possible," January 20, 1997. www.news .cornell.edu.
12. *New York Times*, "In Praise of Tap Water," August 1, 2007.
13. John Roach, "Plastic-Bag Bans Gaining Momentum Around the World," *National Geographic News*, April 4, 2008. http://news.nationalgeographic.com.

CHAPTER 6

At School and Work

Many of the same principles discussed in Chapter 3: Daily Living at Home also apply at school and in the workplace. The individual can take numerous small steps to reduce waste in any setting, but at school or at work the individual usually cannot act alone to bring about broad, institutional changes. Working with decision makers, however, individuals can help enact programs that institute environmentally friendly policies outside the home.

Reducing Kitchen and Lunchroom Waste

Reducing waste in the lunchroom or cafeteria has the immediate benefit of sending less material to the landfill and into recycling, and the long-term benefit of raising awareness among participants. Individuals can make a difference in their own actions and by lobbying for institutional changes at their workplace or school. If lunches are brought from home, they will make the least environmental impact if carried in a reusable lunch bag, if all food containers are reusable, and if a cloth napkin and stainless steel utensils are used. Furthermore, workers can make a difference by keeping their own mug at the office. Even though it will need to be washed, it will reduce energy and waste from using throwaway paper, foam, or plastic cups. After three thousand uses, a mug requires thirty times less solid waste and causes sixty times

Getting Rid of Trays

Cafeteria trays pack a double hit to the environment: not only does a tray need to be washed with soap and hot water, it allows a diner to carry more food than he or she might reasonably eat, thereby increasing waste. Some schools have decided to do away with them. In a study at the University of Illinois, trays were eliminated from a dining hall that served an average of 1,300 students per day. The university reported that not having them saved 516 gallons (1,953 liters) of water a day (110,940 gallons in an academic year) as well as 473 pounds (215 kilograms) of dishwashing detergent in an academic year. There was also a 40 percent reduction in food waste in the dining hall studied—because students could not carry as much, they did not take more than they could eat.

In a May 2009 article on school lunchroom waste, *The Christian Science Monitor* reported that Aramark, a food-service provider for some six hundred institutions of higher education, conducted a survey of twenty-five schools that found that trayless dining reduced waste by an average of 25 to 30 percent. When it asked 92,000 students at three hundred colleges about getting rid of trays in cafeterias and dining halls, 75 percent said they were in favor of the change.

less air pollution than equivalent drinks in throwaway cups. In other words, if a person uses and throws away three thousand disposable cups (which is a cup per workday over twelve years), he or she is adding up to thirty times more solid waste and sixty times more air pollution to the environment than they would have had a reusable mug been chosen instead. To put this in perspective, a company that employs three thousand people who choose to use a mug instead of a disposable cup can have this positive environmental impact in just one working day and a smaller company of three hundred employees in just ten working days.

Cafeterias on the campus of San Diego State University have joined other schools and colleges across the United States in banishing lunch trays. The ban saves water, food waste, and detergent. AP Images.

On an institutional level, students or workers can campaign for programs that improve recycling and reduce waste in lunch rooms. The amount of waste—plates, cups, napkins, plasticware, and so on—in a school or workplace cafeteria is substantial and can be dramatically reduced in cafeterias that use washable dishes, utensils, and cups instead. If a cafeteria is not equipped with such items, biodegradable versions of disposable items can be used. Plates and bowls made from 100 percent bagasse (sugarcane fiber that remains after extracting the juice) have the advantage of being biodegradable, compostable, and made from a renewable resource. Utensils made mostly of corn-based resin are available. Cups are available made of either bagasse, for hot drinks, or corn-based resin, for cold drinks.

Paper and paperboard are the largest component of municipal solid waste—34 percent of all waste that is generated by the U.S. population.

As part of a plan to implement waste-reduction changes in a school or workplace, guidelines need to be established ahead of time, including the decision as to whether the program is to run on particular days or every day. To highlight the difference in waste generated on a reduced-waste day versus an ordinary day, all discarded materials should be weighed and the results published online in the school or company newsletter. Routine trash audits will provide the data that is needed for comparison. The organization Waste-Free Lunches reports that one school-age child using a disposable lunch bag generates an estimated 67 pounds (30 kilograms) of waste per school year; the impact of going waste-free at school can be determined by multiplying this number by the number of students who eat lunch in the cafeteria or luncharoom.

Classroom and Office Waste

When launching a recycling program at school or work, paper is a good starting point. Schools and offices are major users of paper, and the EPA reports that paper and paperboard are the largest component of municipal solid waste—34 percent of all waste that is generated by the U.S. population. The paper industry hopes to recover through recycling 60 percent of the paper

Americans consume by 2012. In 2008 a record-high 57.4 percent of paper used in the United States was recovered for recycling, so the 60 percent goal seems achievable. But even though people are recycling at home—87 percent of American homes had access to curbside or drop-off paper recycling in 2008—relatively few schools and businesses encourage recycling.

In May 2004 the Michigan Department of Environmental Quality's Environmental Science and Services Division published "Reducing Office Paper Waste," a brochure for guiding individuals and businesses through waste-reducing tips and for setting up recycling programs. The brochure includes the following facts about paper use, waste, and recycling:

- A typical business office generates about 1.5 pounds of wastepaper per employee per day.
- Financial businesses generate over 2 pounds per employee per day.
- Nearly half of typical office paper waste [consists] of high-grade office paper, for which there is strong recycling demand.
- It is possible to significantly decrease the costs of buying office paper by reducing paper use and reusing the paper you have.
- Eliminating office paper from your waste stream can cut your waste bill by 50 percent or more.
- Recycling one ton of paper typically saves $25 to $30 in landfill disposal costs and about 6.7 cubic yards of landfill space.
- Commercial and residential paper waste accounts for over 40 percent of waste currently being landfilled.
- Every recycled ton of paper saves approximately seventeen trees. Also, it saves approximately 462 gallons of oil.
- Recycling paper reduces the air and water pollution from paper manufacturing.[1]

RECYCLING RATES OF SELECTED MATERIALS, 2008

Material	Recycling Rate (%)
Auto batteries	99.2%
Office type papers	70.9%
Yard trimmings	64.7%
Steel cans	62.8%
Aluminum beer and soft drink cans	48.2%
Tires	35.4%
HDPE natural (white translucent) bottles	29.3%
Glass containers	28.0%
PET bottles and jars	27.2%

Recycling Rate (%)

According to the EPA, recycling has gone up dramatically in the United States since 1960, when only 6.4 percent (5.6 million tons of materials) of all waste was recycled; in 2008, the overall recycling rate was 33.2 percent (82.9 million tons of materials). Much of this increase is credited to curbside recycling, with approximately 8,660 such programs existing nationwide as of 2008. But, as this bar graph shows, many recyclable materials are not making their way into bins. Office and school participation in recycling programs is essential to increasing the recovery of waste material, especially paper and beverage cans and bottles.

Source: "Recycling Rates of Selected Products, 2008." U.S. Environmental Protection Agency, www.epa.gov/osw/basic-solid.htm.

Tips for reducing paper use in the office and at school include distributing documents electronically instead of as hard copies whenever possible, communicating via e-mail, editing and proofreading documents before printing, single-spacing documents, printing on both sides of the page, and limiting printouts to the exact number needed for hard-copy distribution. Tips for reusing paper include setting aside special cartridges of draft paper (paper that has only been printed on one side) for printers and copy machines and using old paper as scratch paper or to make memo pads.

Every classroom and office should have a receptacle to collect recyclables. Positioning it beside the trash bin makes it easy for everyone to recycle maximally. Educational programs (including field trips to the municipal recycling center), posters clearly showing what to recycle, and regular updates in an online newsletter raise awareness about the program.

The Michigan Department of Environmental Quality outlines the following steps for setting up a paper recycling program at work or school: (1) appoint a recycling coordinator or small team to act as the liaison between management/administration and employees/staff/students; (2) determine what is recyclable; (3) identify where the paper will go to be recycled; (4) design the program, including how recyclables will be collected and informing participants of the guidelines; (5) implement the program, which includes ongoing communication and educational efforts; and (6) monitor the results to make sure they align with goals.

Choosing Recycled Paper Products

Businesses and schools use massive quantities of paper towels, toilet paper, tissues, and printer paper. Purchasing recycled products whenever possible reduces the carbon footprint of the organization. Individuals can make a difference by working with management and administration to achieve this goal. The environmental impact of buying recycled paper products is discussed more fully in Chapter 3: Daily Living at Home.

Powering Off

As in the home, computers, monitors, desk lamps, printers, and copiers should all be powered off at the end of the work or school day. Lights and heating and cooling equipment should also be adjusted at the end of each day. If there are not guidelines in place for powering off, contacting the office manager is advised. Custodial staffs should also be included in the guidelines. In addition to conserving energy and reducing greenhouse gas emissions, powering off will save money for a business, organization, or school.

Growing a School Garden

A school garden provides hands-on education about soil, plant life, water resources, and the environment. KidsGardening.org, a Web site sponsored by the National Gardening Association, reports that, internationally, tens of thousands of schools have gardens, greenhouses, and schoolyard habitats that enrich learning through gardening. The site highlights K–12 gardening projects and allows users to locate other school garden projects in their area to share interests and insights.

Changes in weather and climate can be understood firsthand through working in a garden—seeding, harvesting, and rotating crops. The Edible Schoolyard garden, an interactive outdoor classroom for students at Martin Luther King, Jr. Middle School in Berkeley, California, was established in 1995 in an abandoned lot. Today it is, according to the Edible Schoolyard Web site, "lush with seasonal vegetables, herbs, vines, berries, flowers, and fruit trees." As in other school gardens, teachers and garden staff work together to link experiences with students' science lessons for "truly integrated experiential learning."[2] The Edible Schoolyard Web site explains that the garden is carefully planned to grow a wide variety of seasonal produce that favors the Bay Area climate, which shifts and changes from season to season. Students at the school have also been able to witness the positive effects of a 6,000-gallon (22,712-liter) capacity rainwater catchment system, helping the students understand issues of storm-water runoff, pollution, and erosion, while providing a real-world application of core mathematical concepts.

Notes

1. Michigan Department of Environmental Quality, "Reducing Office Paper Waste," May 2004. www.deq.state.mi.us.
2. Edible Schoolyard, "The Garden." www.edibleschoolyard.org.

CHAPTER 7

Activism

The social activism of the 1960s produced the now well-known phrase "Think globally, act locally," which has been applied to many causes, including the environment. Individuals who measure their own choices against a framework of global awareness can have a positive impact because these choices, however small, add up. The next circle beyond the individual is family and friends; the increasingly larger circles are community (neighborhood, school, work, or faith community), city or town, state, region, nation, and world. Individuals can choose to work in any of these arenas to raise awareness and bring about change. Grassroots efforts begin at the community level and often grow in influence over time.

Consuming Wisely

In U.S. President Barack Obama's inaugural address, he stated that Americans can no longer "consume the world's resources without regard to effect."[1] Later in 2009 his administration signed into law the American Recovery and Reinvestment Act, which included several incentives to encourage consumers to use less energy. What the act did not cover, but can be read into the president's first message, is that consumers can minimize their environmental impact—demand less of the earth's resources—by buying fewer things. Every item that is purchased, whether it is clothing, school or office supplies, furniture, decorations, household items, or electronics, has a carbon footprint. It required natural resources to make, package, transport, warehouse, and deliver to the store where it was bought, and emissions were released every step of the way.

Creative Reuse One way to consume less is to reuse what is already at hand. Finding new uses for old or disposable items requires a little creative thought and in some cases a little time—but probably less than it would take to find and buy a new item. New uses for old items include cutting apart a paper bag to use for a child's art projects, using a worn sock as a dust rag, melting old crayon stubs into new crayons in new shapes, converting worn-out bed linens to rags, and using old jars to store household items such as rubber bands, cotton swabs, pens, and pencils.

Sharing Reducing the number of things that are owned makes a favorable environmental impact. Not only do fewer products need to be manufactured, but the raw materials needed to make them are saved, the packaging materials are spared, there are no transport costs, and emissions are reduced. Live Neutral, a community enterprise of the San Francisco–based Presidio School of Management, provides this tip: "If you only use your tent, ladder, or video player once in a while, consider lending it to others. Some communities have a shared tool shed. Workplaces have book exchanges. Or, you and a friend can team up to buy rarely used items."[2] The Web site Swaptree allows members to trade their media (books, music, videos) with other members for only the price of the postage. Although this practice does create a carbon footprint due to shipping, existing items recirculate rather than accumulate or end up in the trash.

Country of Origin: Knowing Where Something Is Made
Products that travel hundreds or thousands of miles to get to the consumer come with a hefty environmental cost, even though

many large corporations are succeeding at minimizing their environmental impact in other ways (such as purchasing green power or carbon offsets). Most products disclose where they were made as well as where the materials in them originated. The closer to home it is, usually the less the environmental impact. In some categories (such as electronics) it may not be possible to find a product made in the United States or Canada. But following a domestic-origin rule can, in most cases, benefit the environment without sacrificing quality.

Organic Products Clothing, linens, and other fabric products made from organic fibers are becoming increasingly common. Certain catalog and online retailers specialize in items made entirely from organic materials. National retailers such as Target and Macy's also feature a limited line of organic bed linens and towels. Because the raw materials in these products were cultivated without synthetic fertilizers, herbicides, or pesticides, usually the associated emissions will be lower than their conventionally produced counterparts. Several cosmetic manufacturers use only organic ingredients.

As with food, however, there are variables to consider when purchasing organic. For example, an organic cotton towel might have originated on the other side of the world, necessitating transport over thousands of miles and releasing emissions through the consumption of fossil fuel, whereas another, nonorganic cotton towel might have been produced domestically. In such cases it is hard to know which has the smaller carbon footprint. But consumers should note that when they buy organic they are voting with their wallets in favor of a more sustainable agriculture. Organic farming and product life cycles (a life cycle takes into account all the variables of a product's production) are explored in greater detail in Chapter 5: Food Choices.

Paying Attention to Raw Materials Choosing products made of renewable materials should be a priority for the environmentally conscious consumer. Paper, cotton, soy, bamboo, and other plant-based materials are all renewable. It is also advisable to avoid certain materials, if possible, especially ones that are petroleum-based—plastics, some cosmetics, and synthetic fabrics. Although wood is a renewable resource, bamboo grows much more quickly than other trees, so if there is a choice between the two materials, bamboo is the better alternative. The California-based business Dax describes itself as the world's largest eco-friendly department store; it is among a growing number of retailers merchandising products made in a sustainable way.

Newsweek's Green Rankings

With scientific consensus that emissions do threaten the climate, in its September 28, 2009, issue, *Newsweek* magazine undertook the not-small task of ranking the environmental responsibility shown by the largest U.S. corporations. As journalist Daniel McGinn explains, "The economic case for going green is becoming more compelling," and causing corporate America to respond even ahead of a cap-and-trade system that would turn companies' emissions into a bottom-line cost. The U.S. government may propose a system (already adopted by some nations) to make companies financially responsible for their emissions; in other words, the more a company pollutes, the more it would have to pay to do so. "Smart companies are working to better understand—and cut—those emissions ahead of new regulations," writes McGinn. The rankings were published with the awareness that they would prompt discussion and stir controversy. The magazine graded five hundred companies across industries, scoring them on a 100-point scale. Computer giant Hewlett-Packard, with a score of 100, ranked at the top. The following were the top ten finishers in a variety of consumer-oriented industries.

Bank and Insurance: Wells Fargo; Citigroup; Travelers; JPMorgan

Recycled Materials Numerous products are made with recovered or recycled materials. Such products are Earth-friendly and may even be carbon neutral, depending on how they are made. For example, if a new scarf is knitted using recovered wool yarn, there is no carbon footprint to the new product, especially if it is made by hand and sold locally. Furthermore, the original garment from which the wool was recovered does not need to be disposed of because it is being reused—which may even be carbon negative (depending on how and where the product is sold and if shipping is involved). There is a growing cottage industry of individuals making new products from old materials; these are products that are not mass-produced but instead are

Chase; Unum Group; Northern Trust; Allstate; U.S. Bankcorp; Ace; PNC Financial Services Group.

Consumer Products and Cars: Nike; Johnson Controls; Avon Products; Procter & Gamble; Estee Lauder; Colgate-Palmolive; Clorox; Whirlpool; Ford Motor; Kimberly-Clark.

Financial Services: State Street; American Express; CB Richard Ellis Group; Franklin Resources; BNY Mellon; Capital One Financial; Morgan Stanley; Goldman Sachs Group; Charles Schwab; Invesco.

Food and Beverage: Coca-Cola Enterprises; Coca-Cola; Brown-Forman; Molson Coors Brewing; H.J. Heinz; General Mills; Kellogg; PepsiCo; Campbell Soup; Sara Lee.

Media, Travel, and Leisure: Starbucks; McDonald's; Walt Disney; Marriott International; Starwood Hotels and Resorts; McGraw-Hill; Wyndham Worldwide; Time Warner; Las Vegas Sands; Darden Restaurants.

Retail: Kohl's; Staples; Gap; J.C. Penney; Macy's; Walmart; Best Buy; Whole Foods; Limited Brands; Target.

Technology: Hewlett-Packard; Dell; Intel; IBM; Applied Materials; Cisco Systems; Sun Microsystems; Sprint Nextel; Adobe Systems; Advanced Micro Devices.

crafted one at a time. Scarves, mittens, and hats are made out of old sweaters; handbags out of old seatbelts; doormats out of recycled flip-flops and tires; jewelry out of repurposed glass and sea glass; belts and purses out of recycled rubber; furniture out of wine barrels; park benches and outdoor furniture out of recycled plastics (polywood is a "lumber" made of 100 percent recycled plastic). As with food, the closer to home the item is made, the fewer emissions in transporting it to the customer, and therefore the better it is for the environment. The Internet offers numerous options for customers to search for handmade items made of recycled materials.

Supporting Green Companies and Other Organizations Many corporations have taken a leadership position in reducing their environmental impact through Earth-friendly policies in the workplace as well as in the manufacturing and delivery processes. There are various rankings of green companies. The U.S. Environmental Protection Agency's (EPA) Green Power Partnership works with a wide variety of leading organizations, including Fortune 500 companies, to highlight their green power purchases as one measurement of a company's commitment to environmental responsibility. Its top fifty partners in 2009 purchased 12.5 billion kilowatt-hours (kWh) of green-power, including biogas, biomass, geothermal, hydro, solar, and wind. Among the familiar names at the top of that list were Intel, Pepsi, Kohl's, Whole Foods, and Dell. The annual list can be found on the EPA's Web site (epa .gov/greenpower). For anyone who is college-bound or wishing to support environmentally responsible institutions, the Green Power Partnership also publishes a list of the top universities and colleges that purchase green power. Another listing of green companies is tallied by *Newsweek* magazine (see sidebar).

Buying Resale Many thrifty consumers have been shopping secondhand stores for a long time, taking advantage of bargain prices. Resale shopping also benefits the environment: Purchased items

U.S. IMPORTS AND EXPORTS, 1992–2009*

U.S. imports and exports of goods have increased dramatically over the last twenty years. As the following dollar amounts show, imports have almost tripled while exports have more than doubled. The movement of these goods across the globe contributes to emissions. In general, products that are made closer to home have a smaller footprint.

Year	Imports (millions of dollars)	Exports (millions of dollars)
1992	536,528	439,631
1993	589,394	456,943
1994	668,690	502,859
1995	749,374	575,204
1996	803,113	612,113
1997	876,794	678,366
1998	918,637	670,416
1999	1,031,784	683,965
2000	1,226,684	771,994
2001	1,148,609	718,711
2002	1,168,002	685,170
2003	1,264,860	715,848
2004	1,477,996	806,161
2005	1,683,188	892,337
2006	1,863,072	1,015,812
2007	1,969,375	1,138,384
2008	2,117,245	1,276,994
2009	1,562,588	1,045,543

*Data are presented on a balance of payments basis.

Source: Bureau of Economic Analysis, "U.S. International Trade in Goods and Services," U.S. Department of Commerce, April 2010. www.bea.gov/newsreleases/international/trade/tradnewsrelease.htm.

get a second life instead of ending up in a landfill. Furthermore, a consumer's need is met without purchasing a new product that would have generated greenhouse gases in its production and delivery. Resale shops can also be supported through donations of clothing, furniture, and household items. National nonprofits Goodwill Industries and The Salvation Army run resale shops, and most communities have their own resale shops, either independents, where goods are sometimes sold on consignment, or local nonprofits such as hospital auxiliaries.

Population growth is one factor in what former vice president and Nobel laureate Al Gore calls the "the clash between our civilization and the natural world."

Reducing Family Size

Population growth is one factor in what former vice president and Nobel laureate Al Gore calls "the clash between our civilization and the natural world."[3] In 2009 the world's population was estimated to be 6.8 billion, meaning the number of people on earth had multiplied four times in a hundred years (the world population was 1.65 billion in 1900, according to United Nations data). Researchers believe the population will continue to grow to more than 9 billion and then stabilize, around the year 2050. Part of the thinking behind the calculation that the population will plateau is that more women around the globe will choose to limit how many children they have. This choice relies on four factors, according to population experts: (1) the education of girls; (2) the empowerment of women to make decisions in society; (3) giving women the means to manage their own fertility (when they have children and how many); and (4) increasing child survival rates. As Gore points out, this last point seems counterintuitive but it has already been demonstrated that as child survival rates increase, people have a natural preference for smaller families. Controlling the world's population is critical so that humans do not outstrip the earth's resources.

Offsets

Once all possible reductions have been made through conservation efforts to reduce carbon footprint, the individual may also invest in offsetting his or her emissions.

Buying CO₂ Credits Carbon emissions that cannot be eliminated by the individual can be offset by investing in projects that reduce carbon. There are several ways to go about this investment in the earth's future:

- Check with local utilities; many offer carbon offsetting programs that allow customers to purchase credits
- Invest in projects that aim to conserve energy
- Invest in alternative energy projects such as solar, wind, hydro, and biofuels
- Patronize businesses that buy CO_2 offsets themselves; see the EcoBusinessLinks Web site for industry-by-industry listings and more information

Planting Trees Because trees absorb carbon dioxide to produce oxygen, planting trees can offset emissions. Critics point out that the many variables involved in tree planting may make it an unreliable carbon offset, however. These variables include years to maturity of the new trees, the question of permanence of the trees, and the species (fast-growing invasive species, for example, should be avoided). Planting and carefully situating a native species in one's own yard or garden is recommended.

Taking the Lead

Beyond assessing one's own environmental impact and reducing it wherever possible, the individual can work for change locally and globally. There are several ways to spread the word about reducing greenhouse gas emissions at the consumer level.

- Organizing small groups (in the neighborhood, workplace, school, church or other religious institution) with the goal of reducing the environmental impact of the participants'

Following page: Planting trees may be a way to reduce carbon in the environment, although critics note that many variables may make the method unreliable. Getty Images for NARS.

daily activities; this is a good way to share tips and ideas on a regular basis.

• Sharing tips and ideas with coworkers and friends on a casual basis. This can be done without being overbearing or imposing one's own views on others: Consumer choices and money-saving matters often come up in daily conversation, and when they do, talking about carbon-saving measures is a natural.

• Advocating environmental change in the community by working with local officials and waste-haulers to make curbside recycling programs as comprehensive as possible; to plant native trees or public gardens; or to provide recycling receptacles beside trash cans in parks, downtown areas, and parking lots, and at athletic fields.

• Using social networking sites such as Twitter, Facebook, and MySpace to spread the word on the importance of individual actions in reducing energy consumption, making Earth-friendly buying choices, and recycling. Linking to organizations dedicated to reducing human emissions and improving the earth's environment is a good way to pass on the knowledge. One possible link is the EPA's Pick 5 for the Environment program, which provides a list of ten options from which to choose and asks the individual to commit himself or herself to those actions.

• Joining a group that is working for change locally or globally.

Resources for Information and Action

There are numerous nongovernmental organizations dedicated to conservation efforts, through projects, advocacy, and lobbying. Donations to nonprofits are tax-deductible. Furthermore, most organizations depend on a large base of volunteers. A listing of some of the most prominent environmental groups can be found in the For Further Research section of this book.

Local, State, and Federal Law

Finally, keeping abreast of news that affects the environment allows the individual to act when relevant local, regional, or national legislation is pending. Concerned citizens can contact lawmakers, send their opinions to local newspapers, join grassroots efforts to get the word out, and, most important, vote. Many local and statewide referenda have environmental impacts. Candidates for office should be scrutinized for their statements about (and, if applicable, voting records on) environmental issues as well.

The Natural Resources Defense Council helps keep U.S. citizens updated on environmental matters. This action group, founded in 1970, combines the grassroots power of 1.3 million members and online activists with the courtroom expertise of more than 350 lawyers, scientists, and other professionals to "safeguard the Earth—its people, its plants and animals and the natural systems on which all life depends."[4] The organization's Web site features an Action Center that lists relevant legislation and policies that are pending. The section also allows users to take immediate action by linking to form letters that will be sent on their behalf to decision makers. The Union of Concerned Scientists also features an area on its site where individuals can express their environmental views to lawmakers.

Putting Thought into Action

Learning about and staying up to date on environmental issues are the first step in creating change. The next step is to allow that knowledge to inform daily decisions, both small (such as the apple that is chosen for a snack) and large (the car that is purchased). Even beyond the consumer choices an individual makes throughout each day, he or she can work toward change by raising the awareness of others. The thoughts presented here are practical ideas that can be used to minimize the individual's footprint on Earth.

Notes

1. "President Barack Obama's Inaugural Address," *The White House Blog*, January 21, 2009. www.whitehouse.gov.
2. Live Neutral, "Share," February 4, 2010. www.liveneutral.com.
3. Al Gore, *Earth in the Balance*. New York: Houghton Mifflin, 1992, p. 223.
4. National Resources Defense Council, "About Us," April 16, 2010. www.nrdc.org.

Glossary

anthropogenic Related to human influence on nature.

arable land Acreage that is suitable for growing crops.

biomass Plant matter that can be converted to fuel.

carbon cycle The natural movement of carbon through Earth's ecosystems.

carbon footprint The carbon dioxide emissions produced by a human activity in which fossil fuel is used as the energy source.

carbon neutral Having no emissions; not adding any carbon to the environment.

carbon sequestration A natural or artificial process by which carbon is removed from the air and trapped in the soil.

CO_2 Carbon dioxide.

compost To convert organic matter to soil suitable for planting.

El Niño A periodic warming of surface waters in the eastern and central Pacific Ocean that causes unusual global weather patterns.

emissions In environmental terms, a gas that is discharged into the atmosphere because of human activity.

Energy Star A program of the U.S. government designed to increase the energy efficiency of businesses and individuals in order to protect the environment.

food miles Distance a food travels from where it was grown or raised to where it is purchased by the consumer.

fossil fuels Gas, coal, and natural gas; nonrenewable energy sources that were created through natural processes, such as the long-term decay of buried dead organisms, and that have a high carbon content.

green building Creating structures and using construction processes that are environmentally responsible and resource efficient.

greenhouse gas (GHG) A gas that absorbs sunlight (infrared radiation) and traps the sun's heat in Earth's atmosphere; can occur naturally or be made by humans; human-made greenhouse gases are carbon dioxide (CO_2), nitrogen oxide (NO_x), methane (CH_4), hydrofluorocarbons (HFCs), perfluorocarbons (PFCs), and sulfur hexafluoride (SF_6).

greenwashing The act of misleading consumers about a company's green practices or the environmental benefits of its products.

GWP Global warming potential; a scientific measurement of the global warming potential of a particular gas; the ratio of heat trapped by one unit mass of the greenhouse gas to that of one unit mass of CO_2 over a specified period (often one hundred years).

ice sheet A mass of glacier ice that covers surrounding terrain and is greater than 50,000 square kilometers (19,305 square miles).

La Niña A periodic cooling of surface waters in the eastern and central Pacific Ocean that causes unusual global weather patterns.

landfill Waste disposal site where solid rubbish is layered with soil.

MSW Municipal solid waste.

offset An activity that reduces emissions to make up for emissions elsewhere.

organic Fruits, vegetables, grains, and fibers produced without conventional pesticides, synthetic fertilizers, bioengineering, or ionizing radiation and emphasizing soil and water conservation and renewable resources; organic dairy products are produced without antibiotics or hormones.

product life cycle The entire arc of a product, from its creation and the materials that go into making it, through its distribution and delivery, to its final use; also includes its ultimate disposal when applicable.

recover To reclaim, save from loss; when used as one of the 4 Rs, it is sometimes substituted with rebuy, meaning to purchase products made of recycled materials.

recyclable A material (such as paper, cardboard, glass, or plastic) that can be recycled.

recycle To process a material in order to regain it for human use; one of the four Rs.

reduce As in reducing consumption; to use less; one of the four Rs.

renewable Derived from an inexhaustible source (such as the sun or wind) or from a source that can be replanted (such as trees).

renewable energy Energy derived from natural sources that are not depleted through use; for example, biomass (plant life), solar, wind, or water (hydro) power.

reuse To repurpose, rather than dispose of, an existing product; one of the four Rs.

waste stream All materials discarded by humans; includes waste that is recovered for recycling as well as compost.

For Further Research

Books

Gary Braasch, *Earth Under Fire: How Global Warming Is Changing the World*. Berkeley: University of California Press, 2009.
Presents an overview of the current state of global warming and photographs of its effects.

Greg Craven, *What's the Worst That Could Happen?* New York: Perigee, 2009.
Reader-friendly guide to understanding the global warming arguments.

David de Rothschild, *The Live Earth Global Warming Survival Handbook*. Emmaus, PA: Rodale Books, 2007.
Describes essential skills for living through climate change.

Brian Fagan, *The Great Warming: Climate Change and the Rise and Fall of Civilizations*. London: Bloomsbury, 2009.
Recounts a period of warming, from the tenth century to the fifteenth century, that changed climate worldwide.

Ross Gelbspan, *Boiling Point: How Politicians, Big Oil and Coal, Journalists and Activists Are Fueling the Climate Crisis—and What We Can Do to Avert Disaster*. New York: Basic Books, 2004.
Argues that global warming is the most important problem facing the world today.

Al Gore, *Earth in the Balance: Ecology and the Human Spirit*. Boston: Houghton Mifflin, 1992.
The first of Gore's books on the environmental crisis, written when he was a U.S. senator.

———, *An Inconvenient Truth: The Planetary Emergency of Global Warming and What We Can Do About It*. Emmaus, PA: Rodale Books, 2006.
Companion book to the well-known documentary film by the same title.

——, *Our Choice: A Plan to Solve the Climate Crisis.* Emmaus, PA: Rodale Books, 2009.
Presents authoritative research on global warming and solutions for stopping it.

James Hansen, *Storms of My Grandchildren: The Truth About the Coming Climate Catastrophe and Our Last Chance to Save Humanity.* New York: Bloomsbury USA, 2009.
The director of NASA's Goddard Institute for Space Studies analyzes the history, science, and politics of climate change, warning that it will be "a rough ride."

Jonathan Isham and Sissel Waage, eds., *Ignition: What You Can Do to Fight Global Warming and Spark a Movement.* Washington, D.C.: Island Press, 2007.
A guide to building the environmental movement for climate change.

Bruce E. Johansen, *Global Warming Desk Reference.* Santa Barbara, CA: Greenwood Press, 2001.
A compendium of research on global warming.

Fred Krupp and Miriam Horn, *Earth: The Sequel: The Race to Reinvent Energy and Stop Global Warming.* New York: W.W. Norton, 2008.
The head of the Environmental Defense Fund (Krupp) teams up with journalist Horn to outline the path ahead for big business.

Bjorn Lomborg, *Cool It: The Skeptical Environmentalist's Guide to Global Warming.* New York: Vintage Books, 2008.
Reshapes the debate about global warming to offer a moderate's approach to meeting its challenges.

Bill McKibben, *Fight Global Warming Now: The Handbook for Taking Action in Your Community.* New York: St. Martin's Griffin, 2007.
Draws on the experience of 1,400 Step It Up organizers in all fifty of the United States to explain how to build the fight in a community, college, or place of worship.

Ted Nordhaus and Michael Shellenberger, *Break Through: From the Death of Environmentalism to the Politics of Possibility*. New York: Houghton Mifflin, 2007.
The authors, known for their controversial 2004 essay, "The Death of Environmentalism," describe a new politics capable of dealing with the global warming crisis.

Stanley A. Rice, *Green Planet: How Plants Keep the Earth Alive*. Piscataway, NJ: Rutgers University Press, 2009.
Documents the ways that plants keep the planet and its inhabitants alive.

Joe Romm, *Hell and High Water: Global Warming—the Solution and the Politics—and What We Should Do*. New York: William Morrow, 2006.
The founder and director of the Center for Energy and Climate Solutions outlines the threats and offers pragmatic solutions.

David Steinman, *Safe Trip to Eden: 10 Steps to Save Planet Earth*. Philadelphia: Running Press, 2007.
Explores the links between environmentalism, conservatism, patriotism, and national security.

Gabrielle Walker and David King, *The Hot Topic: What We Can Do About Global Warming*. Boston: Mariner Books, 2008.
A concise guide to global warming's problems and the solutions.

Ernesto Zedillo, ed., *Global Warming: Looking Beyond Kyoto*. Washington, D.C.: Brookings Institution Press, 2008.
A compilation of expert opinions from around the world on the current state of the environment, the science, and the road ahead.

Periodicals

Sharon Begley, "Climate-Change Calculus," *Newsweek*, August 3, 2009.

———, "We Can't Get There From Here: Reduction of CO_2 Emissions and Energy Use," *Newsweek*, March 23, 2009.

Ben Block, "Climate Change Will Worsen Hunger, Study Says," *World Watch*, January-February 2010.

Kevin Conley, "The First Secretary of Climate Change: Steven Chu, the New U.S. Secretary of Energy, Is a Nobel-winning Physicist and an Unabashed Advocate of Fighting Climate Change. But Can He Negotiate the Political Realities of Transforming the Energy Economy?" *Popular Science*, July 2009.

The Economist (U.S.), "Touch Wood; Climate Change and Forests," December 19, 2009.

———, "Why Farms May Be the New Forests; Agriculture and Climate Change," January 2, 2010.

Robert Goodland and Jeff Anhang, "Livestock and Climate Change: What If the Key Actors in Climate Change Are Cows, Pigs, and Chickens?" *World Watch*, November-December 2009.

Fred Guterl, "Iceberg Ahead," *Newsweek*, March 1, 2010.

Elizabeth Kolbert, Annals of Science, "The Climate of Man—I," *New Yorker*, April 25, 2005.

———, Annals of Science, "The Climate of Man—II," *New Yorker*, May 2, 2005.

———, Annals of Science, "The Climate of Man—III," *New Yorker*, May 9, 2005.

Alice McKeown, "Coral Reefs Under Threat," *World Watch*, January-February 2010.

Newsweek International, "By the Numbers: Ready for Action (The Public's Opinion on Climate Change Policy)," December 14, 2009.

Prince of Wales, "Green Alert," *Newsweek*, December 14, 2009.

Barrett Sheridan, "What the Future Is Worth," *Newsweek International*, December 14, 2009.

Craig Simons, "Climate Summit's Big Failure," *Newsweek International*, January 18, 2010.

Roger D. Stone, "Change in the Air," *Washington Monthly*, July-August 2009.

USA Today (Magazine), "Global Changes Threaten Millions," December 2009.

——, "Vast Human Migrations Seem Inevitable," August 2009.

Bryan Walsh, "It Will Pay to Save the Planet," *Time*, May 25, 2009.

——, "A River Ran Through It," *Time*, December 14, 2009.

——, "Why Are Scotland's Sheep Shrinking?" *Time*, July 20, 2009.

Internet Sources

The Brookings Institution, Climate Change, various articles, www.brookings.edu/topics/climate-change.aspx.

The Guardian, Climate Change, various articles, www.guardian .co.uk/environment/climate-change.

New York Times, Science: Topics: Global Warming, various articles, topics.nytimes.com/top/news/science/topics/ globalwarming/index.html.

New Yorker, The Political Scene, "Elizabeth Kolbert and Peter J. Boyer Discuss Recent Attacks on Climate Science," February 11, 2010. www.newyorker.com/online/ online/2010/02/15/100215on_audio_politicalscene.

PBS NewsHour, "What Is Global Warming?" March 17, 2009. www.pbs.org/newshour/indepth_coverage/science/ globalwarming/explainer_update.html.

Web Sites

Alliance for Climate Change (www.climateprotect.org)
   Founded in 2006 by former vice president and Nobel laureate Al Gore, the group has more than five million mem-

bers worldwide; it is a nonprofit, nonpartisan organization committed to educating the global community about the urgency of implementing comprehensive solutions to the climate crisis.

The Climate Project (www.theclimateproject.org) Another group founded by Gore in 2006, The Climate Project is a nonprofit with a mission to educate the public and to raise awareness of the climate crisis at a grassroots level worldwide.

Conservation Foundation (www.theconservationfoundation .org) Established in 1972 by business and community leaders, the Conservation Foundation is a not-for-profit land and watershed protection organization.

Conservation International (www.conservation.org) Founded in 1987, CI builds on a foundation of science, partnership, and field demonstration to empower societies to responsibly and sustainably care for nature for the well-being of humanity.

Earth Policy Institute (www.earth-policy.org) EPI was founded in 2001 by Lester Brown, founder and former president of the Worldwatch Institute, to provide a plan for a sustainable future along with a roadmap of how to get there.

Earthwatch Institute (www.earthwatch.org) The organization (founded in 1971) engages people worldwide in scientific field research and education to promote the understanding and action necessary for a sustainable environment.

Environmental Defense Fund (www.edf.org) Founded in 1967, EDF partners with businesses, governments, and communities to find practical environmental solutions.

Greenpeace (www.greenpeace.org) Founded in 1971, this activist group aims to "bear witness to environmental destruction in a peaceful, nonviolent manner."

Intergovernmental Panel on Climate Change (www.ipcc.ch) Established by the United Nations Environment Programme (UNEP) and the World Meteorological Organization (WMO) to "provide the world with a clear scientific view on the current state of climate change and its potential environmental and socio-economic consequences."

Leopold Center for Sustainable Agriculture (www. leopold .iastate.edu) Iowa State University's research and education center established to develop sustainable agricultural practices that are profitable and conserve natural resources.

Live Neutral (www.liveneutral.org) Founded in 2005 as a community enterprise of the San Francisco–based Presidio School of Management, Live Neutral is a grassroots organization that aims to enable individuals to stop global warming. The organization offers several online calculators for determining the CO_2 output of a home, a car, or air travel.

The Nature Conservancy (www.nature.org) Founded in 1951, the group describes itself as "the leading conservation organization working around the world to protect ecologically important lands and waters for nature and people."

The Pew Center on Global Climate Change (www.pewclimate .org) A nonprofit, nonpartisan, independent organization founded in 1998 with the mission to "provide credible information, straight answers, and innovative solutions in the effort to address global climate change."

Resources for the Future (www.rff.org) Founded in 1952, RFF was created at the recommendation of William Paley, then head of Columbia Broadcasting System (CBS), who had chaired a presidential commission that examined whether the United States was becoming overly dependent on foreign sources of important natural resources and commodities. RFF became the first think tank devoted exclusively to natural resource and environmental issues. The nonprofit and nonpartisan organization has conducted independent research (rooted primarily in economics and other social sciences) on environmental, energy, natural resources, and public health issues.

The Sierra Club (www.sierraclub.org) Since 1892, when it was founded by naturalist John Muir, the Sierra Club has been working to protect communities, wild places, and the planet. It is the oldest and largest grassroots environmental organization in the United States.

The Union of Concerned Scientists (www.ucsusa.org) Founded in 1969 at Massachusetts Institute of Technology (MIT), the group is now an alliance of more than a quarter million scientists and individuals. The science-based nonprofit works for a healthy environment and a safer world by combining independent scientific research and citizen action to develop innovative, practical solutions and to secure responsible changes in government policy, corporate practices, and consumer choices.

U.S. Environmental Protection Agency (www.epa.gov/climatechange) Government information on climate change indicators, science, greenhouse gas emissions, health and environmental effects, climate economics, regulatory initiatives, and climate policy. Also, sections titled What You Can Do and Climate Change for Kids.

World Resources Institute (www.wri.org) Founded in 1987 as a center for policy research and analysis, today the WRI aims to "move human society to live in ways that protect Earth's environment and its capacity to provide for the needs and aspirations of current and future generations." The organization's work falls into four categories: climate protection, governance, markets and enterprise, and people and ecosystems.

World Wide Fund for Nature, formerly the World Wildlife Fund (www.panda.org; www.wwf.org; www.worldwildlife .org) One of the largest environmental organizations in the world, the WWF was founded in 1961, "the product of a deep concern held by a few eminent gentlemen who were worried by what they saw happening in our world at that time." The group runs more than 1,300 conservation projects around the world, most of them aimed at bringing about change at the regional or local level.

Worldwatch Institute (www.worldwatch.org) Founded in 1974, the institute is an international research organization aiming to provide research to decision makers in order to create an environmentally sustainable society that meets human needs.

Index

About the Author

Rebecca Ferguson is a writer and editor whose previous reference works include *The Handy History Answer Book* (Visible Ink Press). She also contributed to the online resource Britannica for Kids. She lives with her husband and son in the Chicago area.